MW00773326

My Pain

for

His Glory

My Pain for His Glory

FINDING VICTORY WITH JESUS

By

Charlotte Hudson

CHARLOTTE HUDSON bencharhudson@yahoo.com

Scripture - all NKJV

Endorsements

My Pain for His Glory really takes the reader into the very fibers of Charlotte's story by weaving her pain with His light right in front of the reader's eyes. With each story, the reader learns deeply about Charlotte's testimony of God. They will feel joy, sorrow, light, darkness, and confusion in finding answers. I highly recommend this book to readers who will see through her stories, their own stories, and how she found His glory through her pain. His hands wove truth through her pain and brought the masterpiece to light so readers could experience healing from within.

—April Tribe Giauque MSED
Author of *Pinpoints of Light: Escaping the Abyss of Abuse &*
Out of Darkness: Find, Fuel, and Live in Your Light

My Pain for His Glory is a collection of captivating stories written by Charlotte Hudson during some of her darkest moments in life. Each page was written from her heart as she struggled to cope with life's greatest storms.

Through her writing, the reader will relate to their own battles. They can see how Charlotte turned her storms into glory for God through her faith. Each page will lead the reader out of their own storm and on to light, peace, and joy.

I recommend *My Pain for His Glory* to anyone who is looking for their path out of the darkness and to living a glorious life with God.

—Louise Pistole, Author of *Discover Your Joy*

Dedication

This book is dedicated to two friends who were my mentors during this painful time— Bonnie Haigler, my blind friend, who was never too busy and always threw me back into the Word, and Mary Chamberlain, my supervisor at Sears in Kentucky, who was my prayer partner and was always there when I called. She was never too busy to listen.

A Note To My Reader

I wrote this book during the most painful time of my life. My father-in-law died in a car wreck in 1987. At the same time, my mother-in-law was told she had only six months to live with cancer. Then, my husband and sister-in-law pulled away emotionally.

It left me codependent on my husband. I thought leaning on him would help with the pain of losing a father-in-law that I loved and that it would help with my loss of a father who was never there as one should be. My absent father was busy downing his demons with alcohol. With each swallow, he'd complicated everything.

My father felt it was numbing and washing away his pain, but instead, it stained and pained me more. It was like I was standing on the shoreline crying out across the alcoholic waves my father swam in, but the roar of that water was more significant than my little voice to shout, and what was the use? My father was drowning at sea, and I was alone on the sideline with drink splatters against my legs.

That realization crashed on me for nearly three years, making my grieving so much more in-depth and leaving me in a complicated mess. My world was turned upside down, and I was headed straight to the bottom. How can one walk uprightly with the Lord when you lack stability, direction, and hope? How can one find God in their extremities?

Well, quite honestly, I had a mind shift. I always knew I could pray and that God was there for me, but I needed to talk and share my pain to get the swirling thoughts out of my head, strengthen my resolve to accept the people around me and cry out in such a way that my words would get past the ceiling to Him.

In that emotional state of being, I turned to a few things to help me cope, and one of them was writing. How can something as simple as pen and paper bring clarity to such a lost soul? Writing out my pain and emotions was like turning on little pinpoints of light through my upside-down darkness. With that light guiding me, I felt the Lord near me—I was not alone and could slowly get through the challenging healing process.

Some might read this book as the musings of a lost soul, and you might be right. Others might read through it thinking, "I wonder how she endured the hand that was dealt to her." And finally, others will read these words and find answers to their questions and healing from their pain—I wrote this book for all of you.

As God's children, we rely on each other as a family would. Yes, some families are dysfunctional—mine included. However, many families are filled with light and love—not because they are free from the heartaches of life, but rather because of them. They turn to their foundation of faith and find the Lord comforting them–as I did. I thank God for my dedication and that, ultimately, I had Him.

Now, as you will read, I am not a *Sage* guiding you to a *three-step plan* on how to overcome your obstacles or even *seven secrets* of how to cope with loss, abuse, or addiction, but you will see as I gained perspective through my pain, of where my heart was at, and answers that came to me as I wrote through the gut-wrenching junk.

My heart and mind have sometimes worked against each other during this writing process. Reading random thoughts and stories as they came to me and through me is not the right way for a reader to understand or experience them, so I had to find a way to categorize what poured out of my deep well of a heart.

Each time I picked up a pen and went to my computer to type it out, I didn't know what would happen. It might be something about scriptures, family, or my dear country. I purged as needed, yet I knew I gave it some functionality so that you, as the reader, could understand it.

With this book, you will notice that it is not in chapters as a traditional book is, but instead in sections, and within each area, there are between one and sometimes eighteen thoughts on the subject. The best way to think of this book is like journal writing or a book of poems.

Each title signals a new thought (or a chapter—if you like). The sections are placed alphabetically in the Table of Contents to help guide you to light.

I intend to show you through your *pain* that *you* can find *praise.* You can get through it all, but only with a relationship with the LORD JESUS CHRIST. You know that there is ultimately no way around it.

Life has these hardships, and you will go through them, but why not with someone who is everlasting and constant? Why not with someone who loves you fully? Why not with His arm around you, yoked together in strength? He is the Way, the Truth, and the Light. And I testify that it is true. Jesus is there for us—us is even a part of his name (Jes**us**), so trust Him to get you through it and heal.

Welcome; it is your time to find this hope and light in your life as I have done in mine. "May God Be With You" is my prayer in His name, Amen.

Table Of Contents

PART ONE – FROM PAIN TO PRAISE

PART TWO – LEARNING WHO WE ARE

PART THREE – ALL ABOUT FAMILY

PART FOUR – GOD'S CREATION

Part One

From Pain To Praise

Dear readers,

As a young child, I grew up with the people around me sharing their hearts and souls with each other. It was how we express ourselves, all of it—including the *dirty laundry*. For good or ill, that was what I knew growing up.

Now imagine meeting a beautiful man, a wonderful companion, someone I knew I would spend the rest of my life with, and yet, in their family, nothing was openly spoken about. *Hush* was the word for the family whether it was said or not—it was implied. Keep your thoughts inside, and never share because it might cause discomfort or pain for others.

Holding that pain inside for decades came to a rupturing point, and when it burst, all I could do was write and write and write about it—this is what you are about to encounter. Life's challenges are here to teach us, but are we willing to learn? What is it that we need to know? Well, that's the mystery—or is it?

Usually, something or an event comes into our life that just wholly knocks us off our direction, destination, or focus. We might be tempted to say, "I think I know what is happening, and I can figure this out." Or we might be so blind side we have nothing to offer because we don't have a clue why it is happening.

These moments/events/situations like addiction, abuse, accidents, depression, or death cause pain, and in that pain, we find our choices of our own power being eliminated until there is only one thing left to do—turn to God, a Higher Power, One that is All-Knowing, our Heavenly Father and His Son, Jesus Christ. That's the solution to the mystery. We must turn away from ourselves and place our trust in God that no matter the circumstances, He is there for us—helping, teaching, holding, comforting, guiding, and carrying us. We all eventually get there in the end.

As we build our Trust in God, we learn that the pain we endured can be shifted into praise, hope, and thanksgiving. How? How is our pain ever going to lead to such hope and light? Because we have Him with us. He will disclose answers to us at the right time. Not in the timing we want, but that is best for us to learn.

Our *Whys* might be answered in a week, a year, or longer, or we may never find out until eternity—and even then, God may choose not to disclose it to us. If I believe that God is all-knowing and that all things shall be for my good, then I will trust him.

As I shared my situation with a dear friend, she said, "Your life reminds me of Job." That made me sit down and think for a while. Job 23:10 reads, "He knows the way that I take." I didn't know the end of that pain, but I knew that Job never turned away from God and that I would stay as well. As I stayed, I started to turn my pain into praise and always toward God the way Job did because I do not know, but I do know that God knows.

Readers, part one is about my wanderings through my wilderness because of deep pain and how that pain became my Psalms. So, poetically,

I share with you my heart and healing. To make it easy to reference, I placed them in Alphabetical order according to the title.

Please note that this journey was one walked through in a fog so that the direction will lead you into familiarness, yet it might leave you feeling a little lost. Don't worry. As the stories connect with you, the fog will lift for you as it did for me, and the Light of God will shine in your direction, giving you hope.

Addictions And Idols

Do not lay up yourselves treasures on earth, where moth and rust destroy and where thieves break in and steal.

—Matthew 6:19

Many Christians live a life and never acknowledge an addiction and idol. As we observe many friends, neighbors, and family, I become aware of the habits and what lures them, and Satan is alive and well.

He goes after the ones who have the potential to live and serve a God, and instead, people love their own God self. They don't like the word humility, which resembles weakness, and they don't like giving up control, so around the mountain they go.

When the pain of life becomes unbearable, they resort to drinking, drugs, buying, shopping, and spending, only to leave them in a much deeper hole. Does anyone have peace the next day from trying to ease the pain? The self-centered *Meism* generation is running at a pace, searching, seeking, for an idol. Maybe a mate who is unequally yoked and perhaps a hobby, maybe an extreme makeover, and that changes the outside, but the ugliness of our spirit remains.

Christians seem to have many of the same struggles because they walk away, let the flesh take our minds, and remove a God who can give the peace and comfort we all desire. The busy life enables an escape that keeps us from feeling the Holy Spirit tug and wanting inside our being; then, we close the door to a life of fulfillment.

Our Idols can be money, houses, jobs, a mate, a child, anything, or anyone whom we spend more time with than with the Lord; it can even be church meetings.

When we do anything with wrong motives and do not surrender our minds, hearts, and souls and let the flood of Jesus come in, we will never have a purpose in our lives. We go down the beautiful wide road and miss the detour to go to the narrow road. We cannot do this for one another. Addictions are strong for attention, drugs, smoking, alcohol, decorating houses, buying clothes we cannot afford, or even family. We try to cover up the stuffed emotions of a hurt past.

When we turn and seek and knock and ask, only then will we take the detour and the road may not be so appealing or impressive, but humility will be a part of our vocabulary, and only then will we have a servant spirit and wash the feet of our brothers, slow down, and hear a hurting heart and a flood of compassion will flood the soul.

Addictions and idols keep people from truth and peace, while all along, Christ wants to be your addiction and wants us to lay it all down and stop and be still, and then Satan loses his hold and power, and light will reveal a Jesus who loves and wants all.

Do You See My Crying Heart

Looking unto Jesus, the author and finisher of our faith, who for the joy set before him endured the cross, despising the shame, and has sat down at the right hand of the throne of God.

—Hebrews 12:2

Do you see my crying heart, or do I smile and hide behind my pain? What happened to the days of Sundays for church and visiting family on a quiet Sunday afternoon? What happened to us is that our father and mother protected their family, and now they are abused, if not physically, maybe emotionally.

We run to the phone and not to the throne. We are the loneliest generation, although we have all the material wealth and things no other age ever acquired. We accumulate all the world has to offer, yet we try to numb our senses; we tune out that small, still voice that cries out to us to turn around and stop what we are doing.

We then have the blow of life that hits us and leaves us helpless, and we have a choice. We choose what the world offers or Christ and the peace that passes all understanding. When we face the pain and let the tears flow, God sees our Godly sorrow, which leads to repentance, but when we keep holding on and not letting go of our control, we spiral downward.

If we would yield, let go, and trust God, we would have the peace we so desperately desire. But, we do not want to let our house get quiet, so we might hear the Master call because we might have to change, so we keep making noises going and going.

We like the worldly toys and material things our flesh desires, so we never reach that place of peace. We would have to lay it all down and sacrifice, so we keep going around the mountain and never come off to the valley of tranquility and peace. Where do we turn when news comes of a death, tragedy, health, or other bad news? Do we think God gave us a raw deal and get angry at a God who wants and desires to comfort, lift, and carry us?

We do not spend the time needed to know this great God we serve, our Creator. Knowing all prophets failed and sinned gives us comfort, but God uses each lesson and each experience to teach us how to live. Yet, we do not want to follow the instructions and believe He is more significant than ourselves.

When each prophet came to their end, they only learned what a Savior our Lord is. We are a society that Satan has used with all his tactics to lure us to work more hours, dress for success and drive, and live in the best, yet peace is still not there. We have all the investments that Dow can hold; we buy and have all the toys, but there is still a void, and even if we know what it is, we will never let anybody know what we seek, so we drink, take drugs and fill these aches in our heart.

As we read obituaries, we realize that we all die alike: rich, poor, spiritual, unsaved, or saved. The only difference is whether we know the Lord and where we will spend eternity. Is it too late then to see we need a Savior? Investments should mean each of us investing in a child's life, in a parent who is sick and in need, the lonely and hurting, and the ones who need a listening ear. We all should want heavenly investments that will last.

Our forefathers were so burdened for their fellow man that they would approach them and ask, do you know the Lord? But we today are afraid of what they will say back to us, plus our life may not reflect our walk with the Lord.

Are we one day going to face our Father and have him say, "Why did you not witness that little one or your neighbors? I sent you to them, and you had an opportunity?" We will not have excuses then. What if our Lord told us, "I don't have time to answer or listen to prayer? I'll heal your child later when I get time." We take it for granted that He is supposed to instantly hear us when we do not stop a moment for Him to thank Him for all His goodness.

We know what is right, but choose our way, not His. Our prayer should be, "Lord, help me find the purpose for my life and help me not to be filled with excuses and put off, writing a letter, picking up the phone to encourage or visit and help me to be your eyes, ears, mouth, and hands. Help me walk the walk, not talk the talk.

Expectations

Delight yourself also in the Lord, and He shall give you the desires of your heart.

—Psalm 37:4

Expectations of another can sometimes lead us to a painful valley. When you are going along in life, and a person you love does an act, or he falls away and acts out beyond our wildest thought, and we then have our heartbreak, we then turn to the mender of the hearts and tell Him our pain and then wait on the Lord.

It is hard to be patient when you are a person who can control a lot of things, but today, Lord, I have to depend on you. Thoughts like the waves of this ocean come back and forth in me, needing to break the bondage that holds the ones I love. I then realize I cannot break it, only you, Lord.

When I watch these, I love to self-destruct and go down the wrong road and will not listen to wisdom. I remember the Prodigal Son who went to the pig pen, started with all that he needed, and used it all up, so I must wait for the pig pen and be there for the little lives who get a taste like an ocean wave of a bit of love and normal in their lives.

"I need you, Lord, to help where I am weak, be bold and be loving, be patient, be there ready when the crack leads to the broken vessel, and you come with the glue."

"I'll be there, Lord, helping you when you need me to help put the glue to a shattered life. I'm depending on you to be on time, for you do not approve of sin, wrong attitudes, wrong choices, wrong acts, and especially hurting little children."

"Lord, as I wanted so desperately to have a normal family and little grandchildren to love and care for, my world has exploded many times, and my unrealistic expectations came crashing in on me, so now, Lord, every day I get up needing a father who loves me and will not tolerate sin and I must allow you as I wait to work in other hearts so Lord here am I helpless not hopeless, impatient, but waiting."

"You, Lord, are the only glue that works and fills up the crack when nothing else works, but you, Lord, again help me as I hear your words, *Wait Upon Me*. So, here I am, Lord, waiting, and as I have done many times before, I will see your mighty hand. I don't know when or how, but I know, I know, I know. Amen"

Groans That Words Can Not Utter

I am numb and badly crushed; I groan in anguish of heart. I
am exhausted and completely crushed.

—Psalm 38:8

We all can identify groans. We have all had valleys when we groan
in our painful thoughts and overwhelming circumstances and life with
its valleys, and we groan internally, and only the Lord hears our cry. We
who know the lord know one who intercedes for us, and even though
our words cannot be expressed, the Lord knows the secrets of our minds.

We smile at each other and hug, yet we cannot express our hearts for
many reasons. One fear is someone needing to understand or maybe not
wanting another with an opinion and a know-it-all attitude.

We are very blessed if we have that one safe person in our life whom
we can be honest with and spill the floods of our soul, one who loves
us, knows our faults and failures, sees us, and remains their friend. This
is what Jesus wants to do with us. Even as believers, we never get to
this place because we all keep running to the human touch to fix our
emotions.

We think if we vent and they agree with us, this will remove the hurts
of our hearts, and all along, they are listening with their wounds and
cannot fill you when they need to be served themselves, so together we

share but never resolve the groans of our soul. We never learn to rise, be still, listen, read the Word, and be honest and authentic with the greatest friend you will ever need or have.

We become self-sufficient, so we prepare for the day, exercising, putting on our attire, eating the correct foods, and drive off and forget all about the one who allowed us to rise, provided you your food and clothes, and gave us the ability to have a car and to drive and forgot without Him you will not go anywhere but in reverse.

We don't want to wait until we have the groans and agony that fill us to the brink before we learn to praise the Lord who loved you enough that He let his own Son die for you. He let His own Son die just because of love. Love is a word lacking today. Love of self we all know and recognize. We will go to the extreme with ourselves.

Denying self, we don't meet many of those people today, and when we do, we describe them in our self-righteousness as weak, or they are too emotional. People around them do not understand that they have sold out to Christ and surrendered to a Lord, and those who are still in the carnal state stand and ask, why don't you get yourself together when they stand full of the world, and we are in the Lord, so a spiritual warfare is declared.

Spiritual warfare is like a brushfire today. We see life out of control for many of our family and friends and look to the warnings and the Eastern sky. He is coming soon, and this is good news because where some do not have hope for tomorrow, let us let them see the hope in us, and may the groans in us be turned outward to them to teach them this Christ we know that overcomes all groans, hurts, and heals those wounds because that is what He gave his life for. Then, we may all learn to turn groans into praise.

Is Your Cross Too Heavy?

Be strong and of good courage, and do not be afraid of them,
for the Lord you, God, He is the one who goes with you. He
wil not leave you or forsake you.

—Deuteronomy 31:6

Sometimes, taking up our cross daily becomes so heavy, and we feel we don't have the strength, but then we become aware I am doing this in my own strength. The Lord told us to let HIM carry it.

Keeping our eyes upon the Lord in this world of confusion and all the natural disasters and our children and grandchildren suffering many kinds of disasters of their own, then behind the rose-colored glasses, we see but stay in denial of the fact that the worldly treasures of our hearts have replaced the ONE who wants to occupy that space.

We all run to jobs to buy homes whereby when we shut the doors at night, the hearts of the children and the spouse, and whatever occupies behind the doors of our lives. It may become a time of family and fellowship or maybe bad news of the day, schools, jobs, and spouses that lead to conflict and anger toward children and spouses, and they go to bed with crying eyes and broken hearts.

This is the end of another day letting strangers raise our children because the job of rearing children is too hard, and then when the caretaker of the problems approaches us, we cry out you fix them, I don't have time, then the blame game begins. We don't want to stop and ask ourselves why this is happening. Maybe I need help to know how to love myself and fix me so I can be a healthy parent and love my children.

We let the days slide by, and in His words, it says, we sow that which we reap, more than we sow. In the old days, the mom and dad tried to teach respect and proper behavior by saying, "I am sorry," blushing because certain words were not used in their houses. They respected older people and people in authority, and now children are growing up with all the toys and modern technology, and Satan is having a field day.

If Satan can attack our children and grandchildren, He has the homes or, might say, houses. More are divorced and living with strangers to our children and grandchildren than ever before. The family unit and the extended family have become a room full of strangers, and then we wonder why they act out in aggression, anger, and out of control.

We have become a society of selfish young adults. We do enough with our children to ease the conscience and ease the guilt, but in all of this, where is God? We read with our children, feed them, and give them the best, and the best is void because where is Jesus in all the giving?

If we fail to let this window of teaching fly by, then we will have young men and women with self-taught behavior and videos, movies, and books that are not appropriate fill their minds and act out what they see.

We stand back and say what is wrong with him or her? I have given them everything they needed. We do not want to face our own hearts and souls and ask ourselves, what is my relationship with my Lord, the creator?

We are very transparent to our children, and our attitudes toward the church and the Lord will be reflected in our lives and our homes.

We want our children to be fixed and let our souls go unfixed. When we reach the end of the road, our heart cries out, and we cannot go back to fix past behaviors we have taught our children. We have to face a God who will hold us all accountable for every deed and act that has been done.

The DNA in each of us are also behaviors where YOUR WORD speaks about the sins of our fathers. Suppose we as a technology society do not stop the race we are running and watch what we fill the minds of ourselves and our children and grandchildren. In that case, movies, the internet, and videos become this generation's BIBLE. They will not know the truth. The truth will not set children free because parents raise a generation of confused children. We are losing our children, which is the most precious of all in the Bible.

If we as little children will come to Him, but it doesn't mention wait until you become an adult and then our hearts are not soft they are calloused to a world of temptation, and unless we teach little children love, respect, tenderness, remorse, blushing once again, and words and attitudes, then we are sending a generation into society to run this country without morals or character.

We wonder why there is so much violence. It is a lost generation who never had parents trying to meet their needs, losing a child daily, and hoping somebody will take up the slack and their responsibility of rearing THEIR child while the child screams out for love and attention.

When they receive attention from the parole officer or do drugs and go to rehabilitation, then maybe we will look at our souls. Perhaps then, on our knees, we stop, repent, admit, and come out of denial taught to us in our homes and society, then we will not be ashamed to say the name of JESUS. It is never too late to call on the name of Jesus.

It Took The Pain For Me

Let not your heart be troubled; you believe in God and me.

—John 14:1

How can we, as Christians, ever experience the true nature of Christ without the pain? We come to a crossroads of how we react and choose: walk with Him through the pain or run away into making wrong decisions, trying to keep our minds off the circumstances with too much to drink or a prescription drug that eliminates us feeling the feeling.

We go to doctors with all the symptoms and want them to give a solution to our problem with a drug when all the time we need to feel the feeling, let ourselves admit our failings and faults, and let the Lord into the crevices of our heart like a cleaning solution so it can erode all the hard stuff that has accumulated through the years. He wants to soften it so we can be clean again.

That is why Christ wants and loves little children; their hearts are fresh and new and pure and pliable, but then life takes its road, and our hearts accumulate a lot of debris, and if we do not clean all the dirt daily, then when Christ wants us to hear with our deaf ears, and we have tuned out His voice of correction.

Whom He loves, which is all of us, He corrects. That is where our stubbornness sticks its ugly head up and says, "I am doing it my way; I don't need Him." So then, when a life event happens, divorce, death, or just hurts, we will not let the one who can give you everlasting healing come in and heal the hurts.

We run, visit, shop, and fill the pain with busyness because if we go into the pain, it hurts for a while. After all, the mirror of our souls is revealed, and we are afraid Christ will make us change into another person, and we are not going to take the chance, so around and around the mountain we go.

We may believe what our parents taught us is our Bible instead of examining it against the Word of God. They were also full of sin and might have been wrong in their attitudes and behaviors. We need to measure the wisdom of the Bible.

In our grown-up bodies, we run around with either our parents teaching our self-taught teachings or someone we looked up to as our role models, and we keep traveling our roads and running into walls that just don't seem to be working. We hit the wall, then make another choice and hit it again; the pain seems eternal and never-ending. Only if we would turn off this world's noise and do like Christ and go alone with Him in the wilderness and hear the still, small voice that speaks of peace.

The only way to this peace is to get to know Jesus in your valley of pain. Don't run when confusion and pain arrive like a new baby and you don't know what to do, so run to Him, run to the word, run to the pain, and let it happen.

Don't try to eliminate it with alcohol, drugs, T.V. videos, and ball-games, but let your soul be quiet in your home, car, or wherever you are. Let the birds sing, see the sun and its warmth, and let your heart feel and know your best friend. He is the one with all your answers to your questions and the pain. He is a great physician. He is the educator, the artist, a storyteller, a friend, a lover, a husband, and a wife. He is your everything and will fill your needs.

We are adults trying to set an example to our children and grandchildren, and what do they see? Do they see someone full of peace and joy, or do they see a frantic skeleton of a man or woman so busy filling up their tank that it leaves the little ones empty?

We indulge our children with all the emotional lack inside ourselves and give them so much. They step out into life, then they cannot deliver to their spouse or family, and then hit the road of despair and defeat and say to themselves, "Why can't I make it like my parents?" And they try hard to have all the toys now instead of seeing it took forty years for their parents to acquire them.

Plastic has given our children a false sense of security and an illusion; I can have it now and pay later, but later comes really quickly. Children are born, then reality comes, and then confusion and stress fill their lives.

All of us have insecurities and failures, fears, and full of those hidden spots behind our hearts. Christ says He knows us like the birds that fall, and every hair on our head is counted, but we think nobody knows, but our tongue reveals, and our choices reveal what kind of fruit we produce. We cannot make an apple tree produce oranges.

We cannot change hearts; only people who say, "I have a problem," then say, "I need to work on myself, spend time getting to know the one follow his roadmap, and stop the blame game, let the pain out to Christ, so he can let in love so that we can love our spouses and family and those around us healthily."

We live in an angry world, angry at everybody who hurt us, angry at all around us; when it is *The Big I*, we are angry at all along. We are locked up with emotions of anger toward people or a person who hurt us, and then when the present world hurts us, we lash out with our offense, which is misdirected anger toward that one who is innocent.

We have never let the pain and hurt have the healing oil of Jesus come in. We allow that hard-crusted heart to accumulate harder and harder instead of standing still and letting the oil flow, feel the pain and let it bleed, give it time; then and only then we as a people will have the healthy love in our hearts for our fellow man.

When we think of the love our mothers and fathers had before us, they never had the material world and all the clamor of malls and plastic, so maybe a fistfight was the conflict in their day, perhaps a drunk, as they were called. The next generation of women went to work and left the home and the children, and now it is history.

When there was nothing, we were so rich in our relationships and love; now, we see those hearts waxing cold as spoken in his word. No regard for life or each other and gain spending time, nursing homes have replaced children having time for parents, and nurseries have replaced a mother caring for her baby.

A family has replaced empty mansions without love and time, churches replaced with bricks and mortar of empty pews, and homes without fathers have been replaced with live-in-boyfriend or sexes of the same, and we wonder why anger and violence have become a society like it is. Satan seems to have won, but Christ writes the last chapter of our life.

We were created for HIM, not designed for ourselves. When we watch the world, it is full of Dr. Phil's people in pain and turmoil, trying to be fixed by humans who just might need healing themselves. We must turn around to the only one who can solve the ache of our heart, and it will never be done until we admit, lay down the denial, be still and feel, and let our eyes see, our ears hear from a Savior who doesn't charge for an hour session and wait until next week to give you the rest.

There are no charges, all is paid in full, it is free, and all we need to do is take the gift, open it, and our life will be changed forever, for GOD IS A GOD OF GRACE. Let there be peace now that the entire world cannot put a price on, but God paid the debt for us by His Son dying on the Cross; it is easy; just believe, and you will find rest in your soul.

Journey With Cancer

But they who wait for the Lord shall renew their strength; they shall mount up with wings like eagles; they shall run and not be weary; they shall walk and not faint.

—Isaiah 40:31

Lord, as I face my Mother's journey with cancer, I watch each day another fact, another. Dr. and another trip, and I travel for the third road with cancer with parents, all different people but all alike with pain. I ask you, Lord, what do I do with all the experiences and the walk with each one?

Do I share with a family who is traveling this road? The Lord says I am teaching you long suffering, love, compassion, patience, and who I AM, so I realize it is not all in vain. I ask the Lord to help me when I am tired and weary, not to complain, and yet there is grieving in my soul I cannot control and yet a peace that does pass all understanding.

One Mother-in-law, who grieved over a husband who was killed in a car wreck and cancer treatments that I carried her to and along the way, fed her food and all my emotional support and tried to help her feel the presence of the Lord and the love that I felt for her. A dove appeared on the window in her hospital room, revealing a supernatural message. I came to take her home, and we all in the room experienced the sight.

I then traveled to Kentucky to be with my Father who had cancer. I was driving back and forth on toll roads, sleeping on floors in the intensive care of the waiting room where I saw the last breath of my father, who experienced Jesus and angels that appeared in the room with my sister and her husband.

The Nail and the Light in the room were all beyond my explanation of what it did to my soul. Nobody understands but the Lord where I have been and what kept me going, only the LORD.

How do I explain to people my journeys with cancer and the supernatural revelation that you have presented to me personally and to my family? Cancer is one of tears, pain, some joy, and a close walk with the Lord, and when my fellow man enters this journey, I will use my experiences to walk with them as they now travel.

It may be my neighbor, my friends, or maybe a church friend to reveal that I am a child of the KING, and maybe I'll be a little comfort for that one and share what HE has done for me.

Words cannot describe the comfort, love, and caring of people around us and food nourishment. I praise you, Lord, for the experience with Our Mother, friends, family, and you, LORD. OUR GOD IS AN AWESOME GOD.

Lord, Come Cry With Me

For we do not wrestle against flesh and blood, but against principalities against powers, against rulers of the darkness of this age, against spiritual hosts of wickedness in the heavenly places.

—Ephesians 6:12

YOU CRY WITH ME when I cry over my losses of parents, children who hurt so deeply, and grandchildren who see adults act out childlike lives. You cried over Lazarus, you cried over your Mother, and Jesus in your Word, it said, "... and Jesus wept."

Your Word says you see all our tears in heaven, so I guess you have a lot of buckets with my name on them. When I am in this circle of people that I love, and the truth and contact cannot be had, I stay in a state of grieving and never get past the memories of the way it was and the now.

Sin does separate from abortion, adultery, lies, and deceit and cover up losing a family all because the truth has been so twisted to cover up the absolute truth. Where can I go but to the Lord? You are a God who turned water into wine and a sea to become dry. And the lame to walk and the blind to see.

I also can trust you for my son's future, so I know you cry with me. You will carry me through my pain so that I may today love those in this circle of family who have gone astray. My prayer is today, Lord, you give me strength and wisdom to live for you, be a witness, and let me be a Lighthouse; I need you, Lord. Amen

Loss Like Job

Brethren, I do not count myself to have apprehended, but one thing I do, forgetting those things which are behind and reaching forward to those things which are ahead.

—Philippians 3:13

I may not have lost ten children, or so much wealth like Job, or boils all over my body, but I have had the pain of loss. I lost my childhood to alcohol and living in a home of conflict. I lost a year of school and lay in bed with sickness, not realizing how close to the end I was. I lost an opportunity to have a wedding and wear a wedding dress to be a queen for a day I never was.

I left Kentucky behind, and all I knew lived with strangers, accepted all my new family, and left a Mother behind who had no family to care for her. *Was I selfish*, I ask myself? I had a home and children, and the loss of a Christian home as I perceived.

I wanted a family who prayed, attended church, and had Christian girlfriends; I wanted Sunday dinners together. Was that an unrealistic expectation?

Anger filled my house, and I was feeling such loss and hurt my grandchildren, and my children were hurting due to divorce, and the hurts were all around. I hurt so deeply because the little girl inside me wanted this big, happy family and closeness and to eat and play together, but it was worse than what I experienced as a child that night. This was

Christmas Eve and such a division, and when I think of all the secrets and love for each person I have had, I am so confused at this world I find myself in—so I hang on to you, Lord.

I know what you have done for me while on this three-year journey of crying in a deep valley. I want to be like Job and hang on to you, God, no matter what my surroundings may be, and love all the way. My battle is yours, not mine to fight, so I trust you, and may all around me learn who you are and learn to trust and know a loving God, and may all my losses be your avenue to strengthen me and teach me and then I can help speak for you and what you have done for me. This is your purpose, right, Lord?

We are to tell others about our valley, so if they do not hear, you take their hearts, eyes, and ears and help them listen.

May your will be done in each one of these I am speaking, and you are the one who knows who I am talking about. May God's will be done and forgive me where I have hurt anyone, so Lord, this is all I can do; take it from here, and I will trust you. Amen

Repeating A Cycle

So Jesus said to them, because of your unbelief, for assuredly,
I say to you, if you have faith as a mustard seed, you will say
to the mountain, move from here to there, and it will move,
and nothing will be impossible for you.

— Matthew 17:20

Why does your life keep repeating a cycle of disobedience? We become like hamsters in our cages, going around and around and going to nowhere. It is either because we don't have the right relationship with the Lord, or we run our agenda making fleshly decisions.

We never have a guard on our mouth that spews out the fruits of our hearts. It doesn't take us long until we get into a conversation with you; we decide about your fruit, which reflects soft and gentle or overbearing and angry.

Suppose we never had a healthy earthly father and mother who should have given us affirmation that we were valued, nurtured us, gave us value, and instilled into us relationship skills. In that case, when we get into our environment, we then don't understand why we have conflict and disagreements, and we cannot control our world because our world is so out of control.

Then, our pain spews with anger because of all the frustration that lies so deeply within. Relationship after relationship and job after job with a cycle of conflict, anger, and disagreements may happen in the family, and never acknowledging the common factor is you. Maybe an injury was done to you a very long time ago and never resolved because you don't want to go there because it hurts so badly to remember.

When we become adults and don't go back, we act out our learned behavior, which affects all around us, including that spouse who loves you so profoundly or children who also repeat your cycle because you will not go back.

We then marry with all the past hurts and look through those rose-colored glasses and want a man to control, or a man who fills the void of your father you never had, and when you cannot control, you go from relationship to relationship trying to fill in the gaping hole you have in your heart. The spouse may be an innocent victim all because of your past, but you never went back or had Christ fix the hurts, so you keep repeating your cycle and never have the peaceful and abundant life the Lord wants you to have.

You can never find *Mr. or Mrs. Right* until *Mr. and Mrs. Wrong* are dealt with. We have become a society with many young adults having children, and if they have a new body made over by many surgeries, re-doing their appearance with a new nose and a new tummy lift here and there, they will never change their DNA.

We think if we have sex appeal, this will fill the void of a partner when, all along, it is Jesus who created the body and gave your DNA, and you keep searching and trying to fill it up with all of the projections of the world that displays what it will take to be happy and fulfilled. Why do we listen to that and not a man of God who tells you good news for your life?

We see young girls and teenagers running to strangers because they tell them they are pretty or lie about their worth to give them that missing link to their soul that needs to be loved. More depression, unhappiness, drugs, drunk drivers, conflict with guns, and taking another person's identity to steal that does not belong to them, all because we are a lost generation and God is being removed like the erosion on a shore. We must put God back into a society that gives them hope and breaks the cycle of a lost generation.

The media gives our children a false image of their bodies and worth. In the emotional life, our little girls and boys must be told that they have worth. The schools across America reflect a hurting generation of children, all when the parents are working, making money and having all their toys, and losing the time of building the life of a child inside their walls, all because self comes first and children are somewhere in the list of priorities.

If your life continually goes on a spiral of defeat and never seems to ever get to a place of peace, then ask yourself, have I, as an adult, faced my behaviors, and am I repeating the cycle of learned behaviors that were learned in the home and was that behavior you learned Godly or was it conflict and anger and abuse.

Our life reveals that we have not dealt with it all, so why hide and deny what others see? You will keep this cycle going even with those little lives in your home because they are learning all of your behaviors, and they will act out your fears, your habits, and your example, so where you think you have secrets, God knows all the secrets of your hearts and mind.

Our self-image may be of a feeling of not beautiful or not good, but God sees you as a creature HE created, and HE did not make a mistake creating you. He let his only SON die for you. That is how much HE loves you, and HE also loves those children in your home.

He wants an abundant life for you, not unhappiness and a continual conflict in your soul. He wants to correct your destructive behavior and all the patterns you were taught by someone who had learned behavior in their dysfunctional home.

We run with a generation needier than ourselves, and then we set ourselves up for failure by making wrong choices. There must be a soul who knows Jesus to reach one who is searching for a life that will never have peace.

All of the surgery of nips and tucks, revealing a body of clothes so men will look upon with a lustful eye and maybe turn a head so we can fill the void that the fathers or the male gender did not give us a child. We act out behavior that we think will provide a quick high that the love hunger tries to fill.

It only lasts for a little while. We never realize the external does not fill the internal, beauty fades, and heads quit turning anymore; what then? We then could go into a depressed state because we have based our emotions on the look of beauty outside and never acknowledged the internal dialogue going on inside. We never wanted to give the reins to our hearts to a Savior and enter a relationship with HIM all because we have never been told, or we just think we know it all and we run our own life; well, is it working?

When we deal with the behavior and stop blaming the past, the one who is a victim in your life today, look at you then and only then can you become the woman or man God created. The mask you wear will be removed one day by Jesus, and all the glitz will be gone, and the quick fixes will not be able to be had; what then?

Are you turning to a prescription drug for a band-aid for your bleeding heart, are you drinking to a blackout, and maybe you won't wake up to reality tomorrow, or are you looking again for another relationship?

If you give your body away to them, you will feel the love and need that your soul desperately needs. We must face our behaviors and stop repeating the cycle, and it will never be broken until you stop it.

We must come to the real reason we are here and that GOD created us, and he will give us all you are looking for if only we would stop and face your pain and our cycle of wrong behaviors and acknowledge our needs to the ONE who will hear you, not tell your innermost secrets of your heart. We have stubborn hearts and make bad decisions because we think we are right. HIS WORD says *that man's ways seem right but lead to death.*

The ways of the Lord are not our ways, and unlike a father on earth you may have had, He is waiting for you, the prodigal son or daughter, to come to HIM and let HIM fix you, not all the other things above. He gives you love, acceptance, peace, a relationship that is not destructive, an abundant life without all the world's glitz, and a purpose.

You are making destructive choices that leave you guilty and confused that plagues your soul. You may not have anyone in your life to turn to trust, but you can TRUST THE NAME OF JESUS. Fathers, Mothers, family, friends, and our environment will disappoint and leave us bewildered, but JESUS never fails you.

Let today be the day the cycle of repeating wrong behaviors be broken so that those around you and the future generation that your life touches may be changed forever; you have that power in the LORD. Are you willing to change the lives of those beside you and your future children and grandchildren? It is your choice.

Tears Of Purpose

God is my refuge and strength in times of trouble; therefore, we will not fear even though the earth is removed and the mountains be carried into the midst of the sea.

—Psalm 46:1

Tears are God's way of releasing our pain, reaching the depths of our soul where no one can reach. They wash away the accumulated pain throughout the years as though we gathered old clothes and never cleaned out the new ones in our closets.

God wants to replace all the old stuff and replace it with his newness of peace, joy, wisdom, and, most of all, his complete love.

Tears are a tool to hammer out the dirt from the stone, which is the sin and land that lies covering up the light that he wants to shine in our lives.

We can never let the light shine if we do not allow the pain in and let the tears flow to wash out the old and let the new take room in our hearts.

The tears clear the room like antiques that new ones have replaced. Christ wants to take the tears of pain, make us dependent upon him, deny ourselves, and submit and obey.

Throughout life, my tears of pain and suffering were part of me, part of circumstances and life with all of its barriers, which only tears and pain could remove and help me cross over to the other side. Like the Red

Sea, we stand on the shore afraid and crying, fearing to cross through the deep waters, or we hold Jesus' hand and walk with him through it, drowning. It feels like, at times, screaming out in our souls.

Lord, you know I cannot swim, and I am drowning, then I hear him saying, "Don't give up, keep on, I will carry you, remember my words. I will never leave you nor forsake you."

My toe touched the other side one day, and my foot came out of the deep waters. I looked the same, but I saw and heard people differently. Then my tears came flooding my soul in praise.

Now, through the tears and deep waters, what do I do now? I then realized my tears were now because Jesus Christ chose me and all my circumstances. By His choice, because He knew I could not go into deep waters all along, I had to trust Him exactly where He wanted me.

I have always needed people, places, and things to fill the void, but now I am not needy. I was sensual, and now I know the spirit of the living Lord. I get up every morning now, knowing that when I cried those tears of pain, that was the Lord's University, my taking the exam, and the day I passed the test, I graduated with honors because He wanted all of me. I was a Christian, but the Lord taught me that people, places, and things cannot replace His presence in my heart.

I had a choice: choose the world or life I live for Him. I am not alone. He is my anchor, so He replaced those painful tears with praise and joy. This was only Christ reaching down in His grace and using my willing heart, and I consider myself rich to know a Lord of Lords and King of Kings.

You have a choice, John 3:16, believe Jesus died for you and accept Him that He rose again for you and you shall be saved and He will do for you for what He did for me.

The Facade

Nor is there salvation in any other, for there is no other name
under heaven given among men by which we must be saved.

—Acts 4:12

We all go to church and wear our new attire and wear our faces and
smiles so no one will recognize the pain in our lives. We find our pew
and open our Bible so no one will see we have a problem. The songs are
sung that make us cry, and we cannot let them see us cry for fear they
will think we are the only ones with a problem, so we race our minds to
a place to stop the crying so maybe we can make it until noon, and we
leave needy again.

The pastor preaches, and it seems the message he looks directly at us,
and we hope we can make it not letting the emotion flow. There are two
people in our churches: one of the world and one of the spirit. The Lord
wrote about Mary and Martha to reveal the two hearts of attitude.

Do we sit at Jesus' feet and feed upon Him, or do we stay busy in the
kitchen, which is the world, and never learn of Him? We never realize
that all of us have pain in our life. Some face the pain with JESUS, and
some run to alcohol, drugs, jobs, people, or things that keep our minds
upon the world so we will not face the real you. Some of us are saved and
will barely get into heaven, but God wants more than that for us.

He wants our houses, jobs, or whatever fills up our void. We are to
feel for our brothers and sisters and feel His presence, feel for the children

hurting and older adults who are lonely and depressed, and be honest with ourselves and our sins. Jesus wants us not to be busybodies but busybodies for Him, not carnal like the Mardi Gras in New Orleans, pretending and hiding behind the mask while the pain resides in our hearts and never gets fixed.

We are God's people, and we walk around and around, never making progress, still on the bottle of milk all because we never deal with the issues in our life that lie so deep within, which is just maybe an incident that happened in school, a childhood event that never left our hearts and minds, but Christ wants that issue, and then our behavior will be Christlike.

Instead of the behavior of the world where no one sees the difference between our belonging to Christ or the world, our sin has accumulated like a ball of yarn that keeps getting bigger and bigger and tighter and tighter, and then when we hit that wall of life, where do we go?

We ask ourselves, what do we do now? Our minds and hearts must be in the same tune, or we will never have the peace Christ wants us to have. This is why we stay busy in the world because the spirit keeps screaming for our attention and convicting us, and we want to do what our will wants in the flesh and keep the heart quiet so it will not make us change. We resolve we do not want to change, and we will not be still and hear the little voice that screams in our ears to turn around and change.

We do not like pain, and it will be a pain to face the mirror and see who we are and to change, so we keep the tears inside and our pain and look to a fellow man and we smile and live just like a computer with a complete database, and when it gets so full, it crashes and so do we.

Friend, before that happens, why don't we program ourselves with the Word of God and find that friend that lasts and listens to your every need and never leaves you, nor does HE disappoint you and will love you when nobody else will?

Our churches then would be cleansed, and we would be soldiers full of power and overcome the weakness that keeps us tangled up with our ball of sin. We have a will, a will to change or remain where we are, and only if we accept this One who died for you, which is JESUS, then and only then will we have *peace like a river* and be rooted so deeply in him that no storm can destroy us, so why do we neglect this gift which is free and yet the gift is never opened, why not open your gift today?

The Light

Indeed, He has borne our griefs and sorrows, yet we esteemed him stricken, smitten by God, and afflicted.

—Isaiah 53:4

What a journey this has been, with reunions, visitors, food, and flowers. It was such a lovely walk. Our Mother and the power of her strength rippled down to neighbors and friends and also in other states. We would not take anything for our walk with you, Lord.

We have had so many acts of kindness and such a time of saying goodbye, and now is the time for you, Lord, to carry Mom and us so that we may yield her to you.

Only you know the last breath, so here we are Lord, yielding to your spirit and letting go of a Mother so you can carry her to Glory. You have now revealed yourself in a very supernatural way with the light.

A neighbor thought we were up working with our Mother when she, for some reason, went to the mailbox at 4:00 am, which she never does. She said, "I started to come over and help you with your Mother when I saw you all working with her this morning at 4:00 a.m." She revealed she saw a bright light, which she described as an overhead light, and saw us lay our Mother in her bed.

We replied that we did not have an overhead light, nor were we working with our Mother at 4:00 a.m. We also revealed that only a night light and blinds were pulled, and then we all stopped and realized it was the presence of the Holy Spirit and his Angels in my living room working with our Mother, getting her ready for Glory.

We knew it was going to be alright for our Mother. Only you, Lord, can reveal yourself, and only you can do the impossible that we could not do for ourselves.

The neighbor then begins to tell her story, which can reach people in the neighborhood, and as we told the story to our friends and neighbors, this was a story for others to have assurance for their death. She was used in a mighty way and had a smile until the end.

She walked the walk of faith and left all around her in amazement at how she could face her limited days with such an attitude and strength. We want all to read this and know they can also have the power our mother had when you know a JESUS who came into her room, put his arms under her, and lifted her to GLORY.

Walk In Death Of Mother

He heals the broken in hearts and binds up their wounds.

—Psalm 147:3

Each morning, I awake with anticipation of the death of a Mother in my own home. It has been a bittersweet walk. The emotional roller coaster is taking its toll on me and my sister. The eating, the surge of energy to walk, the look of struggling to breathe, the smell of cancer and its sting of death is a hard journey for us all.

Until you walk this valley, no one can tell you what it is like day to day out 24-7, watching, waiting, and thinking that this is the day. God, in his mercy and grace, is our refuge and strength.

He said He would not put more on us than we can stand, so we trust HIM in the valley again. We are allowed to go deep in the valley to learn about His love and mercy, and oh, what a SAVIOR.

You are Lord, and we love and trust you all the way. We have watched two parents die, but your Mother is different. You always are working to make her better and comfort her like she did us when we were children. Lord, we don't want to lose our Mother, but we do not want to continue thinking of her dying and lying in a bed every day. This is not our Mother who lies confused and cannot move. However, she will never give up and goes beyond what a woman can.

We love her so much and hope when we face death, we face it with such strength and courage as our Mother. God grant peace to our Mother and us, and may your strength and power come into our bodies to lift us higher and higher. May God get all the Glory and Great things you have done and will do. Amen

What Are You Hiding Behind

Yet in all these things, we are more than conquerors through
Him who loved us.

—Romans 8:37

Are you hiding behind a cloth of religion, a uniform or suit, and service to others, and we don't know you at all? When the doors are shut, we really do not know one another. It is based on trust, and we hope you are who you say you are, as we call you by name.

Do you go to the websites, or do you drink until the problem fades into a blackout, or abuse a child or wife and husband, yet we put on our masks and smile as we enter the workplace or place of worship.

When we become aware that God is a God of rules and He created you and gave you the breath you breathe in your body, and yet you live independently, thinking you are your own man or woman to rule the universe in your mind of deception.

When all other options fail, and the trap you fall into will not let you escape your hole, then will you call the name of Jesus, or will you make false promises? When your pain has faded, you repeat your cycle of wrong behavior?

Trust is being lost in our world because we now become a victim in our society. A generation ago, we would help a man with his broken down car, we would let a stranger ride, we would leave with unlocked doors, and now, in the light of day, we all walk around with eyes opened wide to our surroundings all because Satan is roaming the streets to devour and destroy that which is good.

The only one we can depend on and trust is JESUS. Trust must be had to finish our journey on earth, and if you do not restore your confidence and receive Jesus, then your deception will lead you to go on a road of no return. Let us who know the natural person to trust let our light expose the darkness so they will have a life of no regrets.

We must speak the truth, watch the choices, keep ourselves free from a world that sends a message of temptation, go to the spirit within our souls, reject all the lures, and not let the lure be like a hook on a pole and get us hooked. Man cannot remove the hook, and only by a miracle can the Lord do.

An attitude about yourself must be one of Love, let go of your anger of the past, and let your soul heal, which only can be done by JESUS.

Where Does Your Pain Lead You?

No temptation has overtaken you to be tempted beyond
what you are able to, but temptation will also make the wa of
escape that you may be able to bear it.

—1 Corinthians 10:13

Does your pain lead you to an escape that only you and you alone know? Do you go to a bottle that only numbs you for a while and then wake up, and you are still there, and nothing has changed, only a headache? Do you seek someone to love you in many of Satan's schemes? Do we seek relationships to fill the ache in our hearts and the loneliness that only JESUS can fill, and no one ever tells us how?

Our churches are full of people who are saved and only have head knowledge and never let it all drop to all the places in our hearts. We sit every week with troubles and pain and keep it all inside, so we do not want to reveal the confines of our hearts because we were taught never to share our stories.

Our fathers and forefathers never knew the word, dysfunction or codependent. They knew about working five days a week without choosing whether to or not. They sincerely believed in their God and honored him on Sunday, and family was a priority.

What happened to this generation? Satan knew he had to take over the minds of God's people, so he lured Mom out of the home. He knew she would like to shop, so he created malls, and now he decides to create computers and draw the children so the minds will not hear what the Holy Spirit is saying, so the family that honored God is gone, and the sacred honor of Mothers and Fathers are gone, and so is Sunday.

This generation has more than ever before, yet the age before us did not have all the material wealth, but they had *time*. They had time to visit, time to quilt, candy pulling, barn raisings of neighbors' needs, and this gave all the fellowship and shared their love and what resources they had.

We have the loneliest generation ever and have it all, yet millions are taking sleeping pills because of no peace, and the problems are increasing. We have big houses, cars, bank accounts, and investments; we have wealth and security in an insecure world. We seek malls, work, or whatever it takes to fill the loneliness of our planet and the hole in our souls that stays void.

We shop, talk on our cell phones, listen to our iPods, drown out that ache, and try to escape the pain and discomfort. We see the flicks and read the books that take us to a place of imagination that helps us flee this boring life we live.

All along, we are running from a God who loves us and wants what is best and tries to escape the Holy Spirit convicting us, so He says, stop and spend some time with ME. I will fill up the hole, and you will not need to search for all those places that leave you empty and will not last. I will give you peace and joy, but we are afraid and want to feel safe like little children.

We never enter the place for all our answers because Satan uses our minds to say, I will have to change into someone I do not want to be, and I like me, and yet inside, we hate ourselves, but we never realize this ONE who can change us and give us all we are looking for.

We fear losing friends and family or a person we can control, all because we do not know how to go to this JESUS. We still carry our programmed life from the little girl to the boy. We want to be accepted and feel secure and safe, so in this insecurity, we feel so profoundly no one can point us to the answer of joy, peace, and comfort and give us healing for our wounds that lie so deep; only JESUS, He will provide you with all this.

He loves, forgives, and comforts us, and we are like animals afraid of being caught because if we get caught, we face the issues we run from, and we don't like pain, so we run and never let JESUS see us. We live our lifetime with all the secrets of our souls and live a life of pain and discontentment all because we keep trying to do it ourselves.

We will live our lives until the end with secrets, pain, insecurity, and trying to have relationship after relationship until we learn that JESUS is the one to have a relationship with, and only then will the emptiness of our souls be filled.

Part Two

Learning Who We Are

Dear Readers,

The world shouts at us to only focus on us—on *ourselves*. Why? Do you feel a daily battle within your heart to care for yourself, your needs, you, you, you first? The world's voice is thunderous on this topic, but is it evident?

Look at the world's chaos: it is self-centered. People focus on their own agenda, greed, time, money, and power. The result of that self-focus is usually poverty, pain, divorce, destruction of the family, and ultimately decimation of society.

Satan searches and destroys, and this concept of taking care of yourself, self-love, and self-care gets twisted in his hands. He always adds the poison that when we drink it, it enslaves us to his power. The world, or Satan, wants you to see only your needs, wants, and desires, whereas the Lord wants you to *know* who you are and learn who you are.

You need to care for yourself or the Light God placed there, but how we do that is like God did. He reached outward to all to save all. If we reach outwardly, we will be saved inwardly.

As a child, I sang songs like "Jesus Loves Me" and "This Little Light of Mine." These simple songs hold the truth of who I am. I am a Child of God—a Daughter of a King. I have His light inside me. I can shine toward all my brothers and sisters and help lead them back to God.

I learned that simple truth when I was young. It enabled me to remember who I was. It was foundational—I am divine, so knowing who I am was more about learning how to help others.

Now, that's not to say that I never fell and got tempted a little as the battle of Satan raged all around me and then tried to get inside my thoughts and dim my light. I've had my ups and downs but never lost my foundation of learning who I was.

Satan wants you to forget your divinity. He places temptations in your path hour by hour to distract you, running in circles, chasing money, power, youthfulness, and illusions of worldly praise that can turn and consume all your light, leaving you in darkness.

Satan sets you on a hamster wheel, depleting you of your precious energy and seeking false fulfillment. You run and run, getting nowhere but exhaustion, distraction, or your next addiction. When you fall out of the cage, you notice your pain, and because that is too much to bear, you numb yourself with vapors, pills, or the bottle, shopping, stealing, or lying. That is not who you are.

I shared in part one how, when growing up, our family shared everything on our minds, hearts, and souls. We were open to sharing and expressing our feelings. Well, you will read a few psalms in this section about how my soul was nearly crushed by the weight of holding it all in—that I was not being true to myself. But my light shone brighter when I remembered who and who's I was.

As you read all twenty-four Psalms in part two, you will feel the depth of my heart as I learned who I was and how I look around the world and plead for family and friends to learn who they are. My heart, I pray, will help you to notice the battle you are in and to choose. God—after all, we are His, and through Him, we are strengthened.

A Weary People

I am weary from my groaning all night, I flood my bed with
weeping and drench my couch with tears.

—Psalm 6:6

Weary is a word we all know well, and we race to the secret thoughts of
our hearts and minds, and our hearts drag us to an elevated imagination
because our bodies become tired and our minds grow weary. Weariness
can carry you to a place of despair and aggression, and we smile and go
to our work and see our fellow man, and we say to ourselves, "I'll not
let them know what is so deeply inside. They think I'm successful and
display June Cleaver, so "I'll disguise myself, not letting them know who
I am."

Some of us can fake it better than others; some of us exercise and
shop till we drop and block out the pain of our souls. We accumulate
those aches until sleep is disturbed, our minds race ahead, and weariness
shows how we look. We see each other's eyes and the body language that
displays our hearts, and we keep trying to escape a Christ who we cannot
escape. We all run to a mountain or ocean; no matter where you go or
what you do, you cannot escape Christ.

Some of us have more battered emotions than others, and some make
stronger and some weaker, so we think if we run to that friend, take a
drink, take a pill, or pay by the hour to empty our souls of the anguish
we have carried around like a prisoner in chains.

We stay chained and in bondage until the day we look into our souls and let the one who has the only key unlock the door. We are like a pool of stagnant water until we let it out and be cleaned by Christ.

Christ brings the disinfectant in and lets the poison out. That poison has resided for so long and brings such pain. Christ creates a flow of His blood, His love, His care, His healing, and peace to fill those raw spots of our hearts. We will come out of it all a new creature, which He died for, so let your body and mind be cleaned today.

You will have the abundant life you seek, and the weariness will be removed. Still, in your stubbornness, you will not allow yourself to feel the pain and cry out to a father who created and loves you.

You think you can block it, but you are spewing out your angry spirit all around you and hurting people who love you. You will have two choices: One with Christ or rejecting Him.

We must get tired of being weary and want to change because only then will Christ, as with the prodigal son, wait for you, and it will never be too late for Him. He is the answer to the weariness of your soul, and don't waste the years trying to learn this lesson and then realize you wasted years of what you should have done all along.

All Different But All Alike

Repent and turn back so your sins may be wiped away.

—Acts 3:19

Today's human race is so far away from our Lord, and yet so much alike we are. We may be white, black, and yellow of race, rich, poor, but as we die, we all die alike with nothing. However, do we know the Lord as our Savior is the issue?

If we have never accepted Jesus, we die with nothing, and our living is in vain. As people, we race to gain our wealth or race to an addiction that, for a brief moment, gives us relief, and yet when that moment fades away, we are left again with the eating inside of a void we are trying to fill.

We accumulate debt, trying to be like all the society that says you need that car, house, and dress. We even go to different relationships that feed our insecurities and hear advice from sick people who continue to make us toxic people.

These are even Christians who fill a void of the sensual world when all along Jesus is standing there speaking, desiring to fill that void, and the clamor and noise of this world tunes him out, and we don't hear or feel.

We let our will take over, and Satan's lies keep sending us down a death road to Christ. He wants to give us life and abundance. We make choices, and it is for self, not Christ, and those choices make us empty, and then we search in exhaustion to fill those voices that scream in our head that say you deserve it; you don't have to take it.

I'm doing what I want to do so the Lord lets us, and then we continue like a child being put into the time-out chair repeatedly. Some learn the rules, others defy those rules, and one day, we will all stand before a loving God, and I believe he will hold us and cry and say I never knew you.

We call and beg then, but it will be too late. "I died for you and suffered for you, and you were so into yourself and would not listen to me."

Society lives like there is no tomorrow, and we will all come to a day when our guilt will raised its ugly head after some wrong choices made long ago. If we make good choices today, we reap goodness and a fruitful life, which will come back around to correct and bad decisions. Like the Father waiting on the prodigal son, our Father is waiting for us to turn around and make better choices, so why not start today?

Are We Like Hamsters?

For in the day of trouble, he will hide me in his pavilion in the
secret place of his tabernacle. He shall hide me; he shall set
me high up on a rock.

—Psalm 27:5

Like a hamster in a cage, we as a people go around and around and go
nowhere, yet in the blink of an eye, another year has passed. And where
did it go, and what did we do with it?

We see a newborn baby and look again, and they are beginning school,
and then we know time slips away. And did we contribute to someone's
life along the way, or did we, in our flesh and self-centeredness, do for
ourselves and join into this generation?

Young adults today are passionate about seeing how many toys they
can buy and are always looking for a quick high that only lasts for a
moment. They think they can get it in many ways, maybe behind a
door with a liquor cabinet and all the selections available, yet the bottle
becomes empty, and so does their life, and the cycle never ends.

Youth jump into their new auto and take off with their children, who
had an instant breakfast, and away they go and give to society the best of
us and leave us empty again. The mothers today want their children for
maybe their fulfillment and their agenda. Young adults never got beauty,
education, and everything in their homes growing up, and they want
their children, but they are not a priority. They let another person fill all

their needs during the day while money is made to buy the home that is never lived in.

We decorate it so our friends and family will be impressed at the success they see on the outside and yet again running on empty inside. We, as females, search for the hole to be filled with a love for our earthly father, which he never served. Maybe he never told us we were pretty, and then we become adults with still the ache inside looking for a prince on a white horse, and we expect them to fill the hole that was left, which is an impossibility for another to do.

Our emptiness needs Jesus, but nobody took the time to tell us. We heap many unrealistic expectations on a male to fill us up where the pain lies deep inside us. We may shop until we drop and decorate ourselves with the latest fashion smile with our makeover, and our soul still aches in pain that we cannot fill.

We look for somebody to care for us, love us, validate our self-worth, and reload the hole with the world's putty, but all along, Jesus can only heal us and fill the gap. The putty of the world cracks, and we still have brokenness that we have been busy trying to fill.

We want our self-esteem in jobs, clothes, houses, and cars, maybe the president of a club or a leader in a church, and we still try to fill the emptiness of our souls. We work hard 24-7 that what is left for the Lord are the leftovers of our day.

We scream at little children all due to stress in our life and not remembering they want us. They do not want the things money can buy; they want us and all of us and the love they so desperately need. Money cannot buy time.

We teach our children if they cannot believe it or charge it, this is a do not wait for a generation. We take trips to islands, trips to the bottle, and try to drown out the little voice that tries to get our attention, but we keep busy and never still hear the voice of Jesus.

As young adults, we do not want to be controlled, so we do not want anybody telling us how to live our life we make the money, and we will spend it our way is the motto of all young adults today. When the pressure of life hits, and the sickness, creditors, and things cannot be controlled, we come to a crossroads and turn to parents, a counselor, or something or someone for comfort instead of the most excellent comforter.

The Lord tells us repeatedly, come to me, and I will give you rest. Lay your burdens on me, and I'll handle the load. If you believe in and trust me, I will remove the mountains, yet we never get to know Him and His promises. When we fail to get to know the one who can fill our hole and our aching soul, we sacrifice a peace that passes all understanding and forget to have the purpose we are here.

We keep hurrying, opening a can, throwing children in the bed so money can be made the next day, and on and on it goes, and we do not understand what makes us so exhausted. We deny that we love money more than the things that are so important and needed, and then we wonder why our life does not go on the right course and why we are an unhappy generation if we have it all.

If we change partners repeatedly, we will find Mr. Right, and they will fill our hole. They may fill our self-esteem, and then we learn the grass is not greener, and we must also cut their grass.

We must stop, look, listen, feel, and see that little boy and girl screaming inside for help and kneel in total surrender to the ONE who can make it alright and feed and fill us up so that people and the world are no longer needed.

He is Lord of Lord and King of Kings. He is the ONE thing you are looking for, and nobody ever told you. Deny yourself and seek HIM; you will find the peace you desire, not in humans but in the Lord Himself.

Are We Too Busy?

Be still and know that I am God.

— Psalm 46:10

Are we too busy today to see the pain in our brother's eye, who just walked past us all because the mall was having a sale and we had to get there first? Do we have a deadline to beat and tell our Brother that we will call you later? Are we too busy to see a nursing home all because we do not want to be reminded that this too may be one of us, so we run to escape the thought?

Do we run to work, maybe not for the money, but to escape and run to shop, run to whatever the world can offer to make the thoughts, all because we do not want to face the root of our problems? Are we too busy trying to drown out the small, still voice that calls and tells us to be still?

We tell ourselves, there is a football game today, a movie I want to see and shop until we drop, and amid all the noise of the malls, cars, videos, and T.V., God waits for it all to become silent, so we go on numbing ourselves with all the noises of our world to fill our minds we can walk in our way and our agenda.

In the Armed Services, they prepare for battle when there is no battle, and so if we do not know a Lord and know his Word and know who HE is, will the war come? It may be too late to fight the battle.

We should prepare our hearts, minds, and bodies to be ready for Satan's schemes, but if our minds and time are occupied with decorating, jobs, vacations, movies, and books, where does Christ fit all this time? When do we ever learn He is the Rock, our source of strength in times of trouble, and He will never leave or forsake you?

Sometimes, we are not still because we face our guilt and shame at that moment, so we choose not to feel the lousy feeling and work hard at staying busy to avoid the cost of looking at the mirror of our souls.

We don't like hearing our spirit say we must change because we control who we are now. We stay in the bondage of our minds that have been programmed by wrong messages, and we act out these behaviors, so we are told repeatedly that He wants to give us a sound mind. If you were in a business and a Computer Programmer came in and gave you the wrong program to run your business, would you accept the information, or would you say, this does not belong here; it does not work?

We never throw out the old program in our minds that does not belong to us, and Jesus wants to give us all his agenda. Then we will be ready for the battle, so why not today order software from Jesus and let him be installed in you so you will have the correct program for this life we are living and then when you are reprogrammed, maybe you will not be too busy in this world we live for yourself and Christ and your fellow man.

Denying Self In A Selfish World

Behold, I am the Lord the God of all flesh; is there anything
too hard for me?

—Jeremiah 32:16

God's Word states, "Deny self, and we are to be servants or have a servant spirit." We never understand this until we understand our pain in-depth, get into the Word, and bring God's perspective. We then may know like the mind of Christ.

How can we have the mind of Christ if we turn on the TV, play the DVD, radio, or whatever makes noise, go to work, come home, and crank it all up again? God, in His still, small voice, wants to be heard. If we are honest, noises keep going because we do not want to face the fact we have a problem.

We are not convinced to change if we keep the noises and busyness going. We like our self-centered lives, which is how we are, so we try to control our destiny. We fear what we will find out about ourselves.

In this generation we live, we have become a self-centered society. Don't bother me with your problem; I don't have time for myself, much less your problem. Time has become a big problem in this generation. Then I will give you what is left of my time. I wash your feet. Are

60

you kidding? Why was denying self and washing feet something Jesus mentioned in his Word?

Sometimes, we learn the hard way about washing our feet or denying ourselves, and some of us never do. We all have expectations about what life will be like when we are young about home, work, marriage, and children. We have mindsets arrived from our past as to what we expect. If we do not get the education or have a nice car to drive or a lovely house, we may become forced in many ways to make sure this is provided to our children or ourselves when we begin our journey.

When all these dreams do not meet our expectations, what? We can feel for our fellow man like Jesus did when he was hurting and rejected, and his friends and people he thought loved him did not, betrayed in many ways, and he did all good for people like we sometimes think about ourselves.

Jesus never went up to anyone screaming in their ear and telling them their faults or tried to correct them in anger, making them feel less of a man; He loved them and only gave them time, time to love them, time to listen to their hurts and past, He never looked or acted self-righteous or with pride, he can, but in humility, He listens, cares, loved and healed their brokenness.

We have all the answers we think, *I'll fix you if you listen, and I will correct you if you hear,* but only Jesus can do that, and it has to begin in our hearts before we can ever have a servant's heart. We must be willing to interrupt and sacrifice less of ourselves and more of Him.

How can this be if we are a person with a clicker in our hand, a car with a noise, highways of people going to work with the focus of the business, a return to the homes starting with noise all over again? When will we ever learn to wash our neighbor's feet, family's feet, or someone's feet because we did not deny ourselves in the selfish world we are running in?

We play golf at a certain T-time, we are to be at choir practice at a particular time, we need to be at work at a specific time, little league games, and so on. Where in all that busy life is denying me what I want to do so I can wash the feet of the hurting sister or brother? Are we selfish with time? Are we denying ourselves, and are we today washing anybody's feet except our own?

Do You Really Have A Friend

A friend loves at all times, and a brother is born in times of adversity. A friend is always loyal, and a brother is born to help in time of need.

—Proverbs 17:17

We all like to be liked, maybe admired, and seek many kinds of friends: those with the same interests, those with a view like us, and those with whom we can be honest. We have fleshly friends, like those who know where the bargains are and where they get their hair and nails done. We also have friends who share the stories of children and grandchildren. Some even party and have a secret life, maybe drink or two.

We have friends we confide in and share secrets with and feel trust in this relationship with that person. There are so many so-called friends we have surface relationships with, but we will not let them in and know the real us and what is going to the deepest level of our being.

There are friends at work and church who attend all activities and are entertained and are with all these different relationships with a big smile and always wanted acceptance and inclusion. We need someone to put their arms around our aching hearts and soothe the hurt within.

We stand in silence, smile, and never communicate our needs to anyone due to pride because our minds are programmed to tell us not to let them know I am not okay, so we play pretend. We have so many different kinds of friends to meet each chamber of our heart with needs.

Each person plays a part in us. One friend cannot satisfy the need that the other can, so we keep going person to person, trying to fill the emptiness with man and continue in our neediness, not understanding what we need is JESUS.

If we have accepted Him, or maybe we haven't, we go around in our flesh looking for someone to love us and be loved; only then, when we get to the end of ourselves and admit we need more than all these humans can give and say within our spirit. I want to change; this is not working. I look to God and say, "Lord, I want you to change me; I cannot change myself, and there is emptiness in me."

Then Jesus will come in, and you may say I already have Him, but you may have Him in your mind and not in your heart because the mind is crowding out Jesus. Somewhere in all your garbage, He may be there, but He wants to clear all the excess waste and be the only one who occupies your mind and heart, and only then will you have an actual real friend; man cannot do this for you.

Expecting Much

Put on the new self-created to be like God in true righteousness and holiness. Put on your unique nature created to be like God.

—Ephesians 4:24

All of us expect too much of one another. When you draw a circle and put a dot in the middle we zero in on the dot which is an example of how we are with each other. We hyperfocus on the problem and not on all the good around us. The circle drawn and the dot in the middle are examples of how we are with each other. We go to the dot when all around is goodness, but our focus is on the wrongs and negative, which is the dot in the circle.

We never stop ourselves in silence and be still without the world's noises and let the thought process begin of the good act done in the kindness of love, self-sacrifice, and words of encouragement because we all hang on to what we did not do. We do not want to sacrifice ourselves or our time, but we expect much from those closest to us to stop and give the attention and labor of their bodies, and we call this love.

Maybe we don't do it the correct way or the way we would because God created us, and the fibers of our souls are not like anybody else. Our behavior and actions display an act of love, and when we find a critical remark from those we love after trying to help, we feel a discouragement that floods our souls.

We are made to feel it was a deliberate act when, all along, it was an overload of the day and our mind. We think in our minds we are still 20-30 something, yet we cannot perform as fast or alert as before because an aging process has begun. Those closest to us cannot see the forest for the trees or see the glass half empty or half full, so this is how we perceive life and each other.

Our own do not accept the aging process for the fears of facing the truth that lies in the core of all our being because it makes us realize we are in the last leg of this race called life and the unknowns that lie ahead. That is why we must focus not on the circumstances of life.

Jesus never expects more than we can do, and He knows our hearts more than those we love around us. He knew us before we were created and had a plan for us. He knows all about our circumstances and our hearts, the mountains, the valleys that we in our flesh cannot go around or over in our strength; that is why we need a Savior.

The only way is to learn who He is, surrender these times of defeat, lean on the arm more potent than the person we depend on in our flesh, and turn to the one who heals, corrects, loves, and is the only one we can rely on.

When family and friends let us down, if only we have enough knowledge and experience of Jesus, we will begin to shed the pain of life like raindrops on a newly waxed car. It will roll off and let Christ and His love strengthen us inside as a physical therapist does for broken bones. Then and only then will we quit expecting those around us to pull up the slack and for each of us to begin to depend on Jesus because He is the only thing who can take away fears, heal us when we are down, speak to our minds and hearts like no other and wants to be number one.

We must realize that He wants us to know who He is, why He is, and where He is, and then peace like water in a stream will become calm and healing to our souls. The old hymn, "What a Friend We Have in Jesus," is true because all else disappoints, and may we come today to a place of seeing good in our fellow man and the blessings he can only give and stop focusing on the dot.

Is Insecurity Your Force?

These are things you are to do. Speak the truth and to each
other and render truth and sound judgment in your courts.

—Zechariah 8:16

Many who we meet and see smile past or greet us have embedded
insecurity and

co-dependency that run through the fibers of their being. Some reveal
anger, a quick temper, or an answer of defense on their lives, or they may
dress in all the latest fashions of the world and stand with a posture that
does not allow any warmth of love to enter.

When they shake a hand or embrace, it does not take long to feel
the stiffness of their soul. Some work long hours to fulfill their worth
or work with giving to fill or display their self-worth and goodness. We
all are actors and actresses on this planet called Earth, but all have a
common denominator: we all need love and acceptance.

We all do self-talk and feel good about how we look or hate ourselves
or say, "I am not worthy. We say I am ugly, I am no good, or I have made
it so nobody will ever hurt me again."

Many phrases we utter under our smiling faces, and we never reveal
or face the truth as long as we do not let a message enter the eyes, ears,
and heart to melt away the crust of denial and when we let a Savior enter
and put the healing oil on the open sores. The crust has been softened

and removed; we then look into the mirrors of our souls and begin to see a new body, one that GOD created for HIM.

It was not created for man. It was first to love HIM, to love ourselves healthily, and to love others, then be used by HIM. All of us have trials and valleys, and we are to use those experiences to help our children, grandchildren, neighbors, friends, and co-workers, but some get stuck and are afraid to take the crust off and have such insecurity they stay locked up in denial.

They will one day be forced by death or an experience that only pain can put each of us to the next level, and this is when the crossroads are before us. Do you take a drug, drink, or the cross? This is what Christ meant when HE said to choose life or death. Insecurity about our destiny and the lack of knowledge about a Savior's love is why the news every day seems more violent.

Many have chosen the wide road and control. They think about their way of life, but when the method of selecting shatters them, and every avenue is tried, will there be a person to tell you about the ONE who died to save you and loves you and be your dearest friend?

Will I be there to tell you so the insecurity will be removed and security in a SAVIOR will be given to you so that when we meet and greet each other, I feel your smile is genuine, your body is warm, not withdrawn, and your hand will reach to me first? Then I will know you have met the SAVIOR, your insecurity has been removed, and JESUS has replaced security.

Is Your Tongue Attached To Your Heart?

And the tongue is a fire, a world of iniquity. The tongue is so set among our members that it defiles the whole body and sets on fire the course of nature, and it is set on fire by hell.

—James 3:6

Do the hurts of your past and the condition of your heart have a string attached to your tongue? As an adult, have you always tried to cover up your heart and keep the boundaries of your soul a distance from your fellow man? Each of us is alike because throughout our lives, we've been hurt and either been taught correct ways or learned behavior to deal with our pain and aches. Maybe we have never seen our wrong behaviors, and we play the blame game; it is their entire fault.

We blame it on all around us, and if we would only come out of denial, we would look at our circumstances and realize there is a common factor: it may be me and you. Could we be self-centered and selfish, and the boundaries keep us from loving and being loved? The past hurts some that they are afraid and get hurt more deeply than others. They freeze in a state of fear, which keeps them bound and never will be honest and authentic, and anger displays the anguish of the heart.

The tongue reveals a hurt, fear, or emotions that have never healed, so never let Christ into those locked doors so the poison can be released. We are like computers, and a virus infects us; we must be shut down, reprogrammed, and begin again. A tongue can be a loose cannon, and it becomes too late for us to put the words back again when it shoots out the message.

The condition of a heart can make a tongue reveal what is hidden so deep inside each of us. We know if you are bitter, peaceful, loving, and arrogant, and in a moment with you, and when you speak, we are aware of your heart.

Our prayer should be, "Lord, put a guard over my tongue and clean my heart so that my eyes will see, and then my mouth will reflect one of healing and a repentant heart and make my heart like you, Lord, that loves and is love." We take our tongues and hearts into adulthood and wait until a person violates our space, and we are like a loaded gun ready to shoot, and maybe it is not even that person after all. Perhaps it is an unresolved issue of the heart and mind that needs renewal from only a Christ who can only heal.

In His words, a sound mind is continually mentioned, and when we daily walk with our family, friends, co-workers, and neighbors, may we let the light of the Lord light up the darkness of our hearts. We will see a need for a forgiving spirit toward maybe ourselves and those around us and let it begin in us so that we love others like Christ loves us.

Maybe we will see our change, feel love again for ourselves, and forgive the one who hurt us so deeply so that we can love that one who is a victim of our past. Let yourself feel love again and take down those boundaries that keep us at a distance because we want to love you, and Christ does, too.

My Heart Grieves For You

Do not grieve the Holy Spirit, in whom you were sealed for the day of redemption, and do not bring sorrow to God's Holy Spirit.

—Ephesians 4:30

My heart grieves when I see you walk with priorities so misunderstood. My heart grieves when you cannot hug me and let me feel the warmth because you have not let go of your hurts. My heart grieves when you think you do not need God and can do it alone.

My heart grieves for you when I see you stay so busy and never stop to let the Lord, like a steak, marinate us to make us tender so we can love HIM and all the more love each other. My heart grieves when I see you not spending time with the little children, and all they know is a daycare.

My heart grieves for little children who suffer at the hands of abuse behind the doors of our homes. We may work beside them, and they smile, and yet, in the confines of each house, we don't know what may be a secret that will never be revealed.

My heart grieves for you when you use the crutch of a drink or pill and think it will make your pain and ache fade away, and for a moment of time, it will, and then realize as you face a new day, the cycle never ends. My heart grieves for you when you pass me by and cannot see the pain in my face or take the time to hear my voice because your schedule does not have me in your time slot.

My heart grieves for you when I see you shop and buy everything a house needs and fail to see you are not investing in a home. We buy clothes that decorate our aching souls so we look like Vogue wants us to look, or maybe because a father left us empty and void, we act out to dress to attract the attention we never received and validate our worth. If we have a slim and trim body, maybe this will give us the attention we so desperately desire and desire love, and it ends up in the form of self-denial and need so great we don't recognize love at all because we do not know how to love.

I grieve for you when there is no self-control of your emotions or a guard over your mouth. You think you can react to others and say all the fullness of your heart, and all along, we never learned God's Word and the difference between our flesh and the world in us and never got rid of the garbage and replaced it with God's plan for our life.

I grieve for you when you keep searching for the perfect man or woman, and you keep marrying, and Mr. or Mrs. Right never comes, all because Mr. or Mrs. Wrong will never find Mr. Right, or Mrs. Wrong.

I grieve for you because you still have anger hidden in the confines of your heart, and when a present-life situation presents itself, you spew your acid over all of us innocent people whom you say you love. I grieve that you have wasted years when you could have known a Lord more than you do, and you never seem to desire His Word, Church, or with HIM personally. I grieve for you because you do not want friends; you withdraw into your shell and want to hide from people who love you.

You may have issues within yourself and the hurts that you are not willing to risk getting hurt again, so you live a lonely life. You have a safe person, and that is all you think you need when, all along, the secure person is JESUS.

I grieve for you when you constantly see others at fault and never your own. You cannot and will not say you are sorry all because your mind is so convinced you do no wrong, but when you lay your head down behind closed doors, do you feel the presence of the Lord?

I grieve for you that I could have been close to you and your very best friend, but you let the things of this world and misunderstandings part us, and time has slipped away, and now you don't need our friendship and all along, you will find out how much I loved you, says the LORD.

I grieve for you because I miss you so much. You gave birth to me and taught me my values, and we spent many days conversing about the problems of the day; the quietness of my home grieves for you. I grieve for you, my Church that never grew and added to the size because the world entered the doors and hearts of your people. We have blinded eyes, and yet we cannot see or hear.

I grieve because of a family of God that needs a revival. My heart grieves that you are in denial and will not stay long enough to face your pain and let it bleed, and then you will have a healing that no man or thing can give.

Will death come, and will we remain with the secret places of our hearts never corrected, and will we then look face to face at Christ with regrets that a wasted life was presented to HIM and all along it could have been so different? Our prayer now should be MORE OF YOU and less of me, Lord.

Our Battle With Self

I can do all things through Christ who strengthens me.

—Philippians 4:13

We all feel, at times, we fight our inner selves and smile and never let our nearest person know the struggle we endure. We are all alike and different in our looks, but we all fight the same battle, which is with ourselves.

Some of us are disciplined, some are out of control, and we never share our struggles. If we were more vulnerable, then we would open our hearts, minds, and emotions and find someone who went before us and is ready to share His story; this would strengthen and give us the hope we long for and assurance that there is ONE who never leaves or forsakes us and is never late.

Suppose we would only be open to change and acknowledge the truth about ourselves, but we keep busy and never face the reality of why we act and react in our behaviors when God repeatedly states. In that case, He wants us to have a sound mind and to repent, ask, and receive, but we want to fill our time with a busy life and wonder why we never have peace.

We will all run, but when the running stops, what then? Life will stop, and then, as we will always face ourselves, we will ask, why didn't I listen? Why didn't I change? Then, we wasted valuable years when the Lord wanted to be your friend. Do we utter, Lord, I surrender, or are you one of those the Lord makes surrender? Face it all now and have the peace we all seek.

Our Hidden Self

Cast all your cares upon Him because He cares for you.

—1 Peter 5:7

We all feel, at times, we fight our inner selves and smile and never let our nearest person know the struggle we are enduring. We are alike and have different looks, but we all fight the battle of self. Some of us are disciplined, and some are out of control, but we never share the struggles; if we were more open and vulnerable, we would open our hearts, minds, and emotions and find someone who went before us and is ready to share their story. It would strengthen us and give us the hope we long for and assurance.

There is one who never leaves or forsakes us. There is one whose promises never fail and is never late. If we could only be open to change and admit the truth about ourselves, we keep busy so we will not face the truth about ourselves, why we act as we do, react, and the behavior keeps repeating a cycle.

God gives us His Word and keeps reminding us repeatedly that He wants us to have a sound mind, repent, ask, and receive, but we want to fill our time and minds with the busyness of life, and then we wonder why we do not have peace. We will all run, but we will never run always.

Life will stop one day, and then we will all face ourselves and ask, why did I not listen, and why did I not change? Then we realize we have wasted all those years.

All the Lord wants is to be honest with HIM and surrender our ways to HIS ways, then we will have abundant life, but many choose death in a direction they keep going because they think they control their destiny, but one day, we all say I SURRENDER ALL.

Put A Guard Over My Mouth

What goes into someone's mouth does not defile them, but what comes out of their mouth, but what comes out of their mouth, that is what violates them.

—Matthew 15:11

Put a guard on my lips, oh Lord. Because of past experiences and pain, I react like a touch of a hot stove. When I see a wrong choice that my children make, I want them to make the right choices and live according to your Word, Lord

You are the Great teacher and physician, and I have been healed, and like a potter with the lump of clay, you have molded and remolded me. I am still on your wheel, Lord, still making me and creating me into your vessel; even when I fall, you still pound me, but lovingly, you use a gentle hand and again to create a design in me you want, not me.

I know you looked down on the creation of earth and dirt, saw me and all my sins, and saw the potential of a diamond, so you took the dirty piece of rock. You took your utensils and created a diamond and are still chiseling, hammering, cutting, and rubbing to get to the inner beauty of a soul you made. Help me today as you hammer me again by what I hear and see.

Create more of you and less of me in me so that my flesh will be in total control. I need your guard over my mouth, so help me by being loving and less selfish and more like you.

I want to be patient and caring and create in me the right spirit and see and hear like you.

It is so hard to live for you because Satan and his attacks are sudden, and I sometimes do not know until it happens, so Lord help me. I need you now, not later, to be a witness and take over and yield myself right now to your control.

Satan Is Alive And Well

And no wonder, for Satan himself transforms himself into an
angel of light.

—2 Corinthians 11:14

Satan is alive and well, running to every home and person, trying to
devour that which is good. We can get so caught up in everyday activities
and dealing with co-workers and family that we momentarily take our
eyes off Jesus. Satan enters a situation to throw us off balance, and our
flesh rises, and before we know it, we are in a place we do not want to be.

When we do not spend time in the Word for encouragement, and our
fellow man is struggling like us, what can rescue us from the snares of
Satan? We must, at those stressful times, look to the one who says, "This
is my battle; do not retaliate nor get even; I will do that for you" so our
self-control goes out the window because we become disobedient and do
it in our strength and the mess just got worse.

The answer to most problems is simple: keep your mouth shut, take
it to the Lord, and tell Him. As I heard a person say, the throne, not the
phone, and we all fail in this area. Resentment, anger, and disregard for
the Lord can get us all in trouble.

We must come back and have a repentant heart. The Lord will handle
the thing or person grieving you, but an angry spirit, jealousy, or self-
centeredness will only lead to a road of destruction. If we would stop and

say to the Lord, you are the one who tears down the mountain, so Lord, I have a hill, and I cannot get over this, so Lord, here take it from me.

When a room full of hearts with hurts along the way, or maybe we have been accustomed to people giving in to us, and we get what we want if we pitch our fits and all of these hurting hurts are together, then this is a setup for the fruits in each heart to raise their ugly heads, and the battle begins.

After being wounded, we ask ourselves, do I want this, or what do I want so badly in this world? It is worth losing my witness and showing my humanness and sin in my heart, so Lord, clean me up again, test me and find any offensive way in me, and help me to come out of the world and back to you and let others see Jesus in me. Amen

Take The Top Off Your Bottle

But all things that are exposed are made manifest by the light,
for whatever makes manifest is light.

—Ephesians 5:13

Our lives reflect a bottle full of good stuff to drink, but inside, we can only be tasted once we take off the top to ourselves. Our lives are like the inside of the bottle that gets all shaken up.

We shake it up so much inside until there is so much building within; we want to take the top off or release the pressure, but we do not sometimes know how. Some of us stay shaken up and fermenting like an apple that makes vinegar. It starts with good fruit, shiny and good, then along the way, it becomes sour and bitter, all because we do not want anyone telling us how to live our lives.

We know how and will not ask for any help. If we were to bake a cake and we do not know how to cook and do not have a recipe, then when we start putting in the ingredients that we think are correct, from our memory of what our mothers and fathers taught us about baking a cake, so we go ahead until the cake does not rise and falls, we then realize all our wasted efforts.

If we only read Christ's recipe and Word, the top could be released, letting God enter our glass like the liquid in our bottle. He wants to pour the good stuff so we can enjoy what God wants us to drink.

We let the inside become so sour and bitter and spew open our bottles until the top blows off, and everyone around us suffers the consequences of our choices. Jesus wants us to enjoy Him, His Word, and to be free of all the additives this world has put inside our bottles. He said in His Word, "Choose the good tree of life, not death, and taste of Him, and He will give us His life inside us."

Are you an apple, or have you become vinegar? Do you follow a recipe and bake your cake without instructions? Choose today a Christ and let him be your recipe for living so HE can take off the top of your bottle gently, and then you will have freedom, victory, and peace in your life and not go around spewing all the bitter fruit from your heart. Is this bottle a reflection of you?

Taking Time

A time to search, a time to give up, time to keep, time to throw away, a time to tare, a time to mend, a time be silent, a time to speak, a time to be born, a time to die, time to plant, time to uproot.

—Ecclesiastes 3:6

We have all heard about taking time for ourselves, and we all take time for *the me*. Yet, do you take time for the One who allows you to breathe, eat, work, and live and blesses you with all of what God provides?

Do you take time to teach the little child the correct words to say and the name Jesus? Do you take time to value your parents, who sacrificed their world for you? Do you study God's Word, or do you make up your own Bible?

Do you take time to look at yourself in the mirror—your soul? Do you face who you are and face the pain of yesterday? And yet, do you take time with the Lord to heal your pain? Do you take time to hear your fellow man and the trials of their life or do you use your time for all you need and fill up your hole and leave the wounded and bleeding?

Do you take time to see the sunrise or sunset or watch a bird and hear him sing, or are you so busy with the clamor of the world and its attractions that lure you to the malls or salons, maybe a facility to keep your age you think on hold?

Do you take time to see your child crying out in many ways for discipline or for love, and it's too hard to work, so you block the signals, and then when adulthood arrives, and it rises its ugly head, it will be too late to make the wrong right between you. Do you have time for a spouse who needs a gentle touch or affirmation of their worth and appreciation for all their efforts?

Do you take time to call that elderly parent or person who has been neglected and cannot move as fast as you, and so you are searching for a soul who can relieve you of your duties so the big *I* will go uninterrupted?

Do you take time to reach out to those not like you or a neighbor or a fellow worker and let them feel a compassion in your heart that radiates the love and care they so desperately need? Do you take time to be alone and become quiet so the Lord of the Lord and the King of Kings can be felt and heard, or do you blast the CD or TV so loudly that Dr. Phil is the direction for your life?

Do you fill your mind with the garbage of the world, or do you fill it with the promises of God so that your twenty-four hour days are accounted for? Did the Lord get any of your time? Our time is more valuable than money can buy, and we spend it so selfishly and think time belongs to us and fail to see who gives us our time.

The Lord gave us time, and in time, He is coming for you and me, so we must examine time. If we are using it all on ourselves, we will one day face a day of regrets, so what are you doing with your time?

The Real Me

Now faith is the substance of things hoped for, the evidence
of things not seen.

—Hebrews 11:1

Nobody knows me like you, Lord. The depth, the secret places of my heart, my thoughts, my fears, and the insecurities of my soul are all known by you. Before I was formed, you saw me, and like a road map, you led me home. You are the captain of my ship and charting my course.

There have been many storms in my life, yet you spoke like times of old, peace be still and then became peace like a river. You are my anchor and resting place. When all things have been altered and what we hold dear has been removed, then and only then can Jesus work in us.

In times like these, we do need a Savior. We never have to wear a mask and hide from you because you see the real deal, unlike our mates, children, and those dearest to us.

There are those of us who will not stop the labor and the clamor of the world, which is Satan's tactics to get our attention diverted so we will not use our purpose of life Christ desires of us.

When we let the idols of our life determine the activities of our day, and there only remains at the end of the day, then we do not have the right sound mind and stillness in our heart that the Lord wants from us when exhaustion and stress leave little to give to the Lord.

If we could only rise from our sleep, down on our knees first, quietness would fill the room, and the still, small voice then can be heard. Only then can we focus on loving the Lord with all our hearts, souls, and minds.

May we as a people return to a God who provides all the things we are chasing around after, and yet sadness fills the hearts of many, and when we reach the ladder of success and buy and accumulate for the future, we realize life, is but a vapor and we find ourselves with sometimes health failing our family and friends and know then what is important about this journey.

The Lord gives us all things, yet we sometimes return null and void. He will never leave us alone behind the mask our fellow man sees. Our hearts cry about loneliness, health, finances, relationships, family, and children, yet let's not tell anybody for fear of rejection. And maybe they will think I am not who they think I am, and on and on the mask goes, not taking a risk. Just perhaps they also have been where you have been. We are all in this game of life and need each other.

Let's not reach the last stage of life and realize why we didn't reach out, call, give support, care, and learn and then have all these regrets of life overwhelm us, as then we realize as we face the end it was just the beginning of a life of wasted years, but it is never too late with Jesus.

Time

Time to fear, time to mend, time to be silent, time to speak, a
tire to tear and a time to mend.

—Ecclesiastes 3:7

As we all use our time, it is either excellent or bad. We will never be allowed to go there again. It passes so quickly, and then we look back and see a life of regrets or fulfillment. We all control when we get up, go to work, what we drive, and where we go, but we cannot control time.

Time is a gift, and we see many using it for their gain and their glory and others forfeiting the world's gain and investing in the kingdom. When we are given 24 hours a day, what portion is self, and what portion is God?

The God most serve is *self*. Do we call a hurting friend or neighbor or visit the sick? Do we study and receive the wisdom of HIS word, or do we pass the time cleaning, shopping, and using our time, and all of it blows away in the wind?

Do we use our time to use our fruit and talent and bury them instead of letting them multiply for the use of others? Do we plan the day for nails, hair, spas, or maybe golf, fishing, and never enter a moment into the presence of the ONE who provided you all the time and all the gifts?

Are we a generation that has allowed all the computer technology to enter our homes that keeps the noise so loud that God cannot be heard? We will have time one day to die, and we cannot control that time.

What we have done with time will be revealed, and there will not be any changes.

It will be reflected in what others say about us, good or bad. If only we would use time telling each other what God has done or is doing, then and only then will we be investing in time and have a purpose for our lives.

It is not to make money and live anyway we want to and never be accountable for our actions. We reap what we sow with our time, and when we reach the age of a senior adult, we slow down and reflect and face what we have done with time.

Did we waste our years doing it our way, or did we invest in those things money cannot buy? It is always possible to spend the rest of our time investing in a Savior; all we need to do is stop, ask, and receive.

Tree Of Life Or Death

Law of the Spirit who gives life has set you free from the law of sin and death because you belong to him.

—Romans 8:2

Satan is still alive and well and lures and devours those before our eyes, yet we know who is stronger than the evil one. Everyone comes someday to a fork in the road and must choose life or death.

A good or bad road is a choice, and many choose the death route. They think they can control their destiny and do not need the Lord involved because they will do what they want. Our choices are the results of relationships where we are today.

When we ignore the Word of God and live by the world, we spiral into bad relationships with destructive behaviors. We have children and then wonder why they are so dysfunctional and do not want to face our giants and the mirror of our souls.

We can turn around and go the narrow road when we acknowledge our bad choices and behaviors. It takes pain and suffering to turn around, and before death comes, my prayer is to turn around before you cannot get out of the snares of the devil and the bondage that holds you.

All of us can reason and find excuses for choosing wrong behaviors, but we all know right and wrong. The Spirit of God tells us that our stubborn hearts will keep us with the lust of the flesh or desires of the world, and some end early in death or beyond help, and then all the regrets leap in, and what could have been as abundant life is one of waste.

God is calling our names: choose life, choose me, listen to me, come to me, and we do not hear the call and do not want to because we don't love ourselves and say I know He cannot love me, so on goes the cycle of no return. Do you hear someone calling your name to turn around, and will you listen to the Master's call?

You are at a crossroads in life; choices of destructive behaviors have been chosen, but good choices and good behaviors can still be had, and all we need to do is call on the name of Jesus and ask. Seek and knock, and He will open the door and lead you down the road of life. Choose life and choose Jesus.

What's Behind Your Door

Ask and it will given to you, seek and you will find, knock and
the door will be opened to you.

—Matthew 7:17

Behind our doors, we all live a secret life, hoping no one will come in
and find out. Our hearts are bleeding and hurting, so we buy the best to
look our best so we can all look like we are dressed for success in this rat
race world. We watch TV and videos and surf the net, go on vacations
to try to escape the reality of what is happening behind each of the doors
to our lives.

We walk out of our homes, putting on the mask and trying to get
through another day, searching for those activities or people who will
numb the feeling of our loss or pain. Life throws us a fastball, like a
pitcher from the mound walloping us. We then feel the pain that floods
our bodies.

We run behind our door, drowning in sorrow from a bottle or reading
that book that is less than moral, to take ourselves too far away places or
just shop until we drop, and as the busyness numbs it for a little while.
We can never escape the spirit that lies deep within, a God knocking at
our door.

We don't want anybody to know, so we don't tell, and we will not
let it show, so we keep walking around and around in the circles of
life. We still keep getting hit by the fastball over and over. As we age,

the pain accumulates, and as we live, it grows just like the silence of cancer in our bodies.

We all put a band-aid on our sore, maybe a prescription drug, another drink, another dress, or perhaps that new something will make us feel better, so we think this will take the pain away.

We are like a little child going to a doctor for a shot to keep us from having a deadly disease. We don't like it, and it hurts, and it is for our good, so it is with ourselves. We don't want to admit our wrongs to ourselves, so we live a lifetime and miss letting God come in and remove the infections, and we use band-aids. If only we would allow God to remove the cancer so all the poison inside could be removed.

One day, we come to a crossroads where there will demand a choice: choose life or death, Christ or the world. Jesus does not want us to wait until then; He wants to come behind our door with us, and like a new spring day, we can open our door and let the fresh air into our souls so love can flow in and out of our door, and maybe love for ourselves will prevail.

In his words, knock, and the door will be opened, and just like the Dr. and the shot, it hurts for a while. It is for all our good, so it is with Jesus. Let Him into our door, and let Him heal you from all the pain that man or bottles cannot reach.

He is the Great Physician, so let Him in completely and let Him heal all our hurts and make you well again. WHAT WE ARE SEARCHING FOR AND THE PEACE CAN BE FOUND IN JESUS, don't put Him under the band-aid; let Him remove the band-aid, and then your sore will heal.

Where Is God In A Speedy World

But I have calmed and quieted myself. I am like a weaned child with its mother, like a weaned child, I am content instead, and I have calmed and quieted myself.

—Psalm 131:2

Where is God in your busy world? We all try to have a home, a job, and investments for the future. Our focus becomes on ourselves and what we can do and have. Is it the job that builds your self-esteem, a car you drive, or the big house?

Do we try to accumulate wealth, sail to an island, eat, drink, and be merry? Where is God? Is it in the latest fashion, nail, and hair salon, and spa so we can hide behind the mask of a hurting heart?

Where is God? Is it in a football team or a chat room to chat for a while to fill up the loneliness for deeply needing a friend? Where is God? Is it in a book that is less than moral to dream about a prince on a white horse that comes and sweeps us away for a love we yearn so deep in our souls? Where is God in a new car that gives us status or power so we can make a statement that says, look at me and my success?

We do not feel successful in the confines of our souls. Where is God? Is HE in secret places that no one knows about, not even family or friends? We hide behind a bottle or video to escape the accumulation of life's hurts so we can for a while numb the pain, but it won't go away.

Where is God? Is it a drug that has us bound so tight that our minds are hurting and we feel there is no way out of the hole? We want to change, but we cannot seem to change in our flesh. Where is God? Is it in a Church meeting, ball games, or our children that occupies and entertains us so we stay busy and exhausted so we will not feel the presence of God?

As much as we do not want to admit, God has been replaced with this world's activities, and where is JESUS in our many activities? We seek safe friends, friends like us, ones who know us and accept the bad and good in us, and this is the way JESUS wants to be with you and me. Jesus will take us, good or bad, never reject us like man, never disappoint or leave or forsake us like man, never tell what we tell him, always love us forever, unlike man, because man is flesh and of the world. HIS WORD says to know the truth, and the truth will set us all free. We must want it and then seek it and ask.

Who Are You

And no wonder! For Satan himself transforms himself into an
angel of light.

—2 Corinthians 11:14

I thought we knew you; your face and name are one I know, but
do you have secrets of the heart? Are you sitting beside me or standing behind me with Satan working in your mind and spirit, and the
unknown is acted out in the secret confines of your soul?

Has the mind become an illusion of thoughts only you know and act
upon while I smile and sit beside you, not knowing the conduct of your
secret life at night?

Do we think our sin will not find us out, and we secretly go to places
our families and friends are unaware of, escaping the fulfillment of our
thoughts of our hearts and minds? Will we not be found out or caught if
we block the signal that screams out to us in a still, quiet voice and walk
away when it says do not do it?

We yield, and then we lose the soul. We become numb in the conscience that so desperately cries out don't go there, don't yield and yet it
is in our stubbornness we go ahead and think no one will know when all
along your Creator is there with you, so you take that drink or that drug
to escape the message that penetrates your soul.

The crust of your heart accumulates like petrified wood, and it all starts
with green wood through the storms, the rain, and the environment.

It hardens little by little, and no matter how much you try to water the hardwood, it is so hard it will never return to the tenderness of the beginning.

Our churches are being reached by Satan's lure and dragging away one by one like the erosion of the sandy beaches, and when the soul falls like a home, the ocean and the waves carry you out to no return, and so is life.

When a life preserver is thrown to you while you are floating in the deep waters, why not grab it immediately when you reach the shore, and you receive the SON with all the warmth, then let Him remove that hard crust, clean up your mind, and remove the desires?

He is in the mending business and the only hope for your broken life. Don't wait until the rescue is beyond limits, and return to the Anchor for your life and use your pain to teach a generation of people where you have been. The Lord is on the shore waiting for you to grab the life preserver; grab hold of the one who can save you.

You Don't Know Me

Brother, if a man is overtaken in any trespass, you who are spiritual restore such a one in a spirit of gentleness.

—Galatians 6:1

We have neighbors, friends, spouses, and family members, but they don't know us. They see our faces and call us by name but do not know us. We grow up with a hidden life and learn behaviors from the environment of our youth, and we are all different but very much alike.

We all want to be accepted, approved, praised, loved, and included in this game we call life. We think I work hard enough, give more, and dress successfully; I'll fit in and be accepted, whether it be Corporate America or just a neighbor or friend. If I attend all the PTA meetings and all the ballgames, I'll be the best parent or please everyone who asks anything of me, so I will receive validation of my worth.

If I put myself on a church committee, I'll use my energy for man, and they will think I am a good person for the Lord. If I buy a big house, drive the latest vehicle, and look successful, then society will think I am climbing a ladder of success, but when that door closes at the end of our day, man does not meet our needs.

You don't know me because I am afraid to tell you I don't want rejection again. I don't want to be hurt again. Maybe some of us were injured by a parent or maybe somewhere words that killed our spirit as a child, so we in our little minds said, "What is the use of trying? I cannot please these *Big Ole Adult People.*" Maybe that teacher or that person in our church failed before us, not living before us as an example of what our young minds perceived a Christian to be.

You do not know me because I fear failing and seeking some help. After all, you will think I am weak, and society labels us. You can't tell me because I may have an eating disorder. I eat emotionally because I cannot express that I may not like myself or my life.

I go to a Doctor with maybe depression, and I've been told by man, "Well, you need more faith, you need more this and that, and if you know the Lord, you would not be depressed," and so on and on it goes. You don't know the deep valley we share, so why use words that keep us all in the valley?

Maybe a hug from you, an affirmation of all my good, just might be what we need that would be better than the medicine from a Doctor's office we just left. Maybe I need your time, perhaps I need you to listen, perhaps I need a visit, a phone call. You don't know me and the bondage I'm in. We want real people, not a mask our faces have. Take that shield off your heart that when I greet you, you are so stiff, I feel no warmth flow from your body.

You don't know me; maybe I am fearful of a critical spirit, and all my fears keep me feeling like I am swimming upstream, and I become exhausted trying to please all those around me because I could not ever please as a child. Maybe you dream of a prince on a white horse, leaving a country town and making a lot of money, then I will be somebody. Then they will love me and appreciate me.

All the hurts and disappointments are like a load of baggage on our backs, weighing us down, and no matter where we go or what we decide, the weight determines the decisions and attitudes of our hearts. We may make decisions for Christ and always try to earn the feeling of *I'm Good*, but we never learn grace.

We face the fast track of life trying to put our ointment on a sore that will never heal and never allow the only one named JESUS to heal our sore. Only He knows our hurts, trials, pain, sorrows, and fears, and when our soul cries out, He hears.

Maybe you say nobody knows me and nobody cares, but there is one who created your heart, your eyes to see, your ears to hear, and He counts every hair every day on your head. He knew you before birth, but life and people damaged the perfectly born child. Could it be your life, your words, and your attitudes that have kept me from sharing my heart? I may be afraid of judgment. Perhaps I am so scared of loss. Maybe I am so afraid you'll think I am not the Christian you thought I was.

We read the Word, but do we understand the Word that speaks of board and speck in our eye? Do you try in your insecurity to remove my spec while a board prevails in your eye to be removed?

When are Christians going to stop? Look, listen, and again, may I say listen. We talk too much, and the world needs a listener to hear the hurts, pains, and difficulties. The reason for alcohol, drugs, and escapes that are used is a crying heart screaming nobody cares, nobody listens, and nobody loves me, so I don't even love myself; I guess I don't have worth.

Are we, as a church and people, so busy that when a little child acts up, we say, why don't they raise their child correctly, and again, in the spec of our eyes, judgment prevails? When do we take time to understand that little child and its environment and circumstances, hold it, and show it a tender heart?

Don't we as adults remember maybe one person in our life who did say that one encouraging word, and we recognize it forever as they stopped, looked, and listened?

Do you want to get to know me is what JESUS is asking us, and if we know HIM, we are to be like Him; then it begins with children, young people, the young married , and so on.

You do not know what's in my heart, only Jesus, but if we stop this running away and see the hurting, lonely, and aching guts, that one you might help might change the Nation.

"I will never leave nor forsake you," says the LORD, so don't forsake the one who knows you better than a spouse or best friend. They are human and man and cannot ever help you like JESUS.

Part Three

All About Family

Dear Reader,

At the time of this publication, many of you reading this might think you understand what a family is. Still, I can assure you that if you don't have a foundation of God, you will only be *playing house,* hoping to bend the rules to your selfish imagination and not place it foundationally on truth.

You might not grasp what a traditional family is since modern society has completely changed and distorted it to the degraded form we find it in. As you read this section, your eyes will take in words, sentences, and paragraphs that describe a *Utopian society* that supported and demanded civility, kindness, and decency.

You might think I pulled these stories or descriptions of family from a 1950s TV show. Rest assured that what I describe is the generation I grew up in. Connections were made in the day as two people chose to love, honor, and serve one another. They knew of their divinity, and with that knowledge, they brought children into their family through the love and power of God.

As children were born, the nurturing and protection of that family were the priority. The society that people raised their children in, as a whole, supported that. I was blessed to be born in such a time. And in my long life, I realized I was held at the tail end of that upbringing.

Looking at the family today, I feel a mixture of sadness, chaos, and fear. It's like people are going through the motions of dating, marriage, and having children—possibly to fulfill the expectation, but they are so lost they don't know why that tradition was set in the first place.

God's plan is simple: boy meets girl, they love and respect one another, decide on marriage, and start a family. They can teach and instruct the children who God is, who they are, and how to love God and their neighbor as they work by the sweat of their brow to provide, nurture, and love one another. The whole of society is trying to do the same, and so it works.

But Satan is cunning and knows that if families remain on a foundation of God, He will never win. So Satan is patient and deceitful and stirs one ingredient that all humanity is weak with—pride. Pride causes a person to think of himself first and foremost, and with that one vice, satan can chip away at virtue and convince whole generations to build families on sandy foundations just like the foolish man did.

Satan has removed God from our society by mingling truth/scripture with deceit and lies. Half-truths are his specialty, and your society is reaping what has been sown by selfishness, narcissism, and pride. All the while, he laughs at the people who feel their way perfectly to the slippery slopes of hell.

Is there any hope? Truth flows through this section if you are brave enough to stand out in society and follow the truth. God will not force any man to heaven. He will leave you guideposts and encouragement through scripture, church worship, and love. If you follow that, you can knock down your pride and, with humility, return to the foundation that families are from God.

Are You Listening To Your Children?

The sacrifice of God is a broken spirit and a broken and contrite heart; these, O God, you will not despise.

—Psalm 51:17

Today's media is full of reports of men trying to abduct children, missing children, etc. Children are not allowed to play outside and be free like the generation before them. We have become a society of prisoners within our own homes. Satan knew if he possessed children, the house would crumble. More sexual exploitation, all the DVD and internet movies have numbed the minds of society and the predators and children in their innocence trust so completely.

Children with the images of the perfect body and all the pop stars try to show skin that makes them feel like they have the bodies to lure the attention they so desperately need. Our children are crying, and where are the parents? Where are we as a society and a church for these children? Jesus' priority was the children; his love for children is revealed repeatedly.

The family is too busy working on their agenda, forgetting that the children are getting the crumbs of life. Where is God, the church, in all the 24-hour days of their life? Adult parents need a Savior and a relationship with Jesus, and then they will want to teach their children that it is not clothes, your body, the money shopping that gives you peace.

When parents have insecurities in their souls and try to lead the children while they drink while they watch ungodly electronic devices, whether internet, DVD, or movies, how will children ever deal with hurts, losses, and depression if parents are not living the walk?

When will parents ever be held accountable when we in society see teenagers with their conscience with no remorse, all because parents have allowed the babysitting of their children in this electronic age of gadgets and all they hear is pop stars and all the songs of this age, and where is the name Jesus in their vocabulary? We ask, "If is it too late," but remember it is never too late with Jesus.

Children Playing

Then they also brought infants to him, and he might touch them, but when the disciples saw it, they rebuked them, but Jesus called them to him and said, let the little children come to me, and do not forbid them, for of such is the kingdom of God.

—Luke 18:16

What happened to the day when children went to grandma's house, men sat around telling tales, women sat at a table sharing their weekly stories, and cousins played in the yards? There was tag, *red rover—annie over*, unknown to a generation today. What happened to us as a family where visiting was a priority, and we sat together, and you knew you were loved by each other?

We never felt the inconvenience of being unwelcome because we were more important than a nap. We shared food, and where there was sickness, we cared for them above our plans for the day and brought them soup from a kitchen without instant meals, all lacking in recourses but not in love.

What happened to men who told tales of their dogs, hunting, and childhood experiences of days of old while children sat in amazement and visual thoughts raced in their heads? What happened to quilts being quilted by a group of neighbors, and fellowship was not one of Dr. Phil's stories or soap opera dramas?

There were gatherings for baptism at a river, and all were praised because a lost family member was then found. The little church had relatives from one generation to another who were taught a behavior to love the Lord, and children all learned the name of JESUS and respect for life.

What happened to those homes where floors could be walked on and not afraid of mud to leave a print, and homes where the food could be placed under a table cloth, all because we knew we were welcome to eat the bread at any time?

What happened to singing on a porch and the old gospel hymns about leaning on the everlasting arm? What happened to Sundays when there were no malls, no one working, only attending a group of saints who loved the Lord and were concerned about our souls?

What happened to 4-H clubs and women who taught children how to sew or men who taught boys to shoot guns only at animals, not humans, because life was valued in every way? What happened to people who have lost their way and profanity was a sin, and morals were a secret that was cherished and taught to their children. What happened to doors not being locked and children roaming free in the fields and running in their environment, and safety was never an issue?

What happened to children running in the fields and yards, not anything but dirt, to fill their jars with lighting bugs or maybe a June bug on a string? What happens to children who do not know how to wade a creek and turn a rock to find a crawfish and are not afraid of his claws and no parent screams with fear to lay them down?

We all remember marbles, hopscotch, skating with a key; what has happened to our precious children? Have iPods, DVDs, PlayStations, and all other devices been replaced for our children and grandchildren where they can never imagine?

We had playhouses and pretended to have a Mom and Dad and baby. Now they have become so confused with the same sexes in their homes, a live-in boyfriend, a mixed family of hers, and theirs. Their little minds cannot even go to any imagination because they are going past childhood into an adult environment that requires them to grow up past the fun as a child, all because of the selfish generation that wants what they want NOW, and kids can get over it.

When children are exposed to violence, TV is less than moral, and they stop thinking like a child. Sex and violence have been introduced into a young mind; then, we are programming a generation of little boys and girls to act out on that behavior. This will come back to bite them.

When children's laughter and games are lost, and the church is never attended and taught the word of Jesus, they become victims to a world of darkness. Now we lock our doors, see who is beside us and behind us, and little children every night and day being abused and abducted, and sex being displayed in many forms, then we know the day draws nigh the coming of the Lord. Pretending to be a mommy or daddy is painful for a child, and they grow up past childhood then the parents must ask their minds, when popping in a DVD to babysit our children, what message are they learning?

When little boys show aggression at an early age, and little girls want sexy clothes so early, then are we asking ourselves, why? When we deny it now, we will pay later in the behaviors of our future generation.

The denial of the young adult parents is all around because the self has replaced the sacrifice made for us with less material needs. Still, we had love; we had time and freedom to be a child and run with children and never lived in the fear someone was going to take us away. Homes without fathers. Mothers, head of the household.

When searching for a relationship to fill the void of the past that will never be had, only Jesus can serve you. The children are looking for security and love.

There must be a lot of millstones around some necks today because God's Word said if you hurt these little ones, you will have a millstone around your neck. So we look at our society and girls and boys being exposed to sex on every corner; there are many hurting children.

Parents must stop the madness and come off their ladder of success. When they get to the top, they will turn around and look—the children are gone. They are not there because you want your agenda. They become victims of the world that lured them to find a false sense of security and love. All they want from you is your time, not money or things that can be bought. Love and time cannot be purchased.

From Generation To Generation

And his mercy in one who fear him from generation to generation

—Luke 1:50

As little children in our grownup bodies, we act like adults; we do adult things, but inside, we are all little girls and little boys trying hard to grow up. We do not realize as we are learning our ABCs, we are also learning the parent's behavior and dysfunction.

We are learning, either good or bad, so we take it into our world and take it everywhere we go. We are secure or insecure; we feel good or bad, alone or whole of life. We love these people who are our instructors, and we grow up thinking this is how everybody lives. We all face our battles and become re-actors just like we have been instructed by a mother or father, maybe both. We feel pain and wounded and wonder why it is not working or did not work at all.

Most of us, who are called Christians, operate from this mindset. We accept Christ, and yes, we will go to heaven, and yet we do not want to go through the journey with Jesus and His school of learning because we just want to stay learning the ABCs over and over, and we remain in our comfort zone.

We do not want to look back and learn of ourselves because nobody likes pain, so we operate from a worldly, self-taught life. God's Word speaks of renewing the mind and breaking strongholds. We have a heart for Jesus but never realize there is a battle for our minds.

We must get our body, soul, and spirit healthy at the same time, and if we do not, then there will be a painful struggle and tug of war inside us that will never be fixed. If we made a pie and were looking at the recipe and left out the eggs, there may be a pie on the outside, but the inside lacks the ingredients to make it like the recipe directed for a pie.

It is just like the Word of God; it is there to instruct us, and we cannot have the life he wants for us, and nothing can be left out, just like the making of the pie. We must take His Cross and Word daily, not the world's word, and we must become still and hear that small voice. If we always talk and listen to the world's message, peace will not be found, and the life we want will not be had.

The accumulation of garbage from our past years is Christ's specialty, and the earthly fathers may have passed down their sins upon us because they are flesh and man. We operate from those learned behaviors, and we must come to a place and ask ourselves, is this working for me?

We all have choices: Christ and His Word, or what the world offers, whether alcohol or drugs, affairs or money. The busyness of keeping ourselves from facing the pain, or we can stop still look at ourselves in the mirror and meet our pain with Him, hold to and believe Him and His Word.

People need the Lord, and we run because we do not have enough of the Word in our hearts, and our minds are so full of the draws from Satan to lure us into places of no return when Christ created you for HIM.

The reason is that Satan controls us, and if we do not have Christ's Word inside us, in our thoughts, attitudes, and behaviors, we will fail. When the storms of life come, and you have not prepared for the battle, then like a tree without roots, you will fall, and you will lose the war, all because your hearts are not grounded in Jesus.

We must ask, seek, and return to the one who loves us enough that HE died for us, and your purpose is not for your pleasure but for Him, and He will not give up until we all live this life He gave us, and we learn of him, and if we don't then, peace will not come to each of us. Let Christ and His Word be your armor; it will be well with your soul. Amen.

Fruits Of The Children

And the Lord will grant you plenty of goods, in the fruit of your body, in the increase of your livestock and the produce of your ground, in the land of which the Lord swore to your fathers to give you.

—Deuteronomy 28:11

Little children touch us all, and we see in your words why you loved them so. They are so innocent, loving, and accepting, yet they leave all that to an environment that rubs them daily. Some are then hardened or taught behavior that becomes bad or good, all because parents and their choices mold people and have lasting effects on society.

The little ones are watching, absorbing, that then reflects a learned behavior in their adult years and the emotions are damaged where parents have got their priorities all out of order.

Jesus is a priority that should be taught and let enter that little one so that when a decision is to be made, right or wrong choices, He is the one who enters the child and speaks in his spirit to say to them you don't steal, you don't cheat, you don't hit, you don't lie and say words wrong toward others, and all along the busy parents are in denial and play the blame game and live their lives and say maybe it won't be noticed.

When the teenage years appear, and the actions reveal reaping and sowing, we lose control, and the war begins. Even when teaching the right things, there will be war between good and evil, but when Jesus is left out entirely, we are setting ourselves up for heartbreak as parents and grandparents, and some decisions we make will be found out.

There will be no hiding or denial, and past regrets cannot be re-captured. While we have time to get up, get our minds off ourselves, take a good look, and see if your past is making you, as a parent, have behavior that reveals your heart and your life is not anchored with Christ, so how can you teach these little ones? He will hold us accountable for this task.

We sow what we reap is very accurate, especially with children, so while they are in our walls, reach down, read, love, teach, forgive, pray, and let Jesus be the controlling force behind your hearts, heads, and mouth and live your life so that when the fruits of your labor are revealed, it will either be a prodigal son or daughter because the actual fruit on your tree will be shown, ask yourself, are you nurturing your fruit inside your wall?

Generations Come And Go

One generation passes away, and another generation comes,
but the earth abides forever.

—Ecclesiastes 1:4

Generations come, and generations go, and we move further and further away from our Creator. We have become so occupied with electronics such as iPods, DVDs, the internet, and all the lures that hook our minds to keep it away from the ONE who created it all. He gave it all, and yet, in our ego, we believe we make money and earned the degree; we deserve the toys.

In today's generation, it is all about *me, myself, and I.* This lifestyle has entered the doors of our sanctuaries and never allows us to change or to reach a world with all this technology and find the greatest friend we will ever need or have.

If we are never *still nor quiet,* and our minds are continually hammered with noise, will we ever *be still* and hear the name of Jesus or the small voice whispering of the still small voice among the noise?

Our grandchildren and children are in every activity to make their bodies and self-esteem elevated, but are we entering in them and their actions the activities that last? Are we giving them the Anchor that will hold them when the storm of life comes? Have we shown them Jesus and planted their roots deep enough to anchor their life to Him? We have the power to help this generation, yet are we?

These kids think to ease the pain should be done with a drug, a cigarette, a drink, or an activity that will numb the pain. They are rarely taught that Jesus is the one to run to. These substances will never fix the hurts in their hearts. They will wake up the next day with guilt and not even know why.

Maybe it's the confusion of their world. There are too many voices, and we have not taught them in all the confusion about who to run to. Maybe because their parents are on their level—still suffering in their pain and not understanding that God is the only one who can save and heal them. Perhaps they still need to be fixed and haven't learned the principles of life.

When it is too late, we hear adult children saying, "If I had only…" yet we are not willing to change and set before them an example of the difference that Christ made in their own lives.

Parents, you must be the lighthouse for the children. You but keep the lower light burning and send the beam across the way when one poor wayward struggling seaman you must rescue you may save. When they are in deep waters and situations and see no light for them, there is someone they will go to—Christ. It is always Him.

We all as people must be held accountable for the life we project to children and grandchildren, and maybe when they are in darkness and cannot find their way, we will be light and lay down our selfish agenda and sacrifice our time, money, and invest in a life where the dividends will bring a return not null and void.

Do we live our life and give our children and grandchildren the fragments of the day and say well, that is your problem; you got into it, now get yourself out, and never teach them how to get out of it? Be honest with yourself when you answer that question.

We do not want to sacrifice time with God and family for our time for the world. But in fear, we will stay busy to block the noise of the one who screams at us in our spirit. Are we like the man? Are we reaching out to those who stand naked and hungry? It is the Word that spoke of seeing the man laying on the side of the street broken, and yet are we walking past him because we choose not to see him, or we are so busy we don't see him?

Do we stop to hear a bird sing? We turn off all the noises and hear the quietness of our houses, the rush of the wind, and feel the presence of a holy God who owns us and all of the gifts He gave us in this life to use.

When they roll you down a hall at a hospital on a gurney and rush toward the physicians who only have limited abilities, then maybe you will call on One who has been there for you all along, and now you will *Be Still* and listen.

Groans That Words Cannot Utter

I am feeble and severely broken; I groan because of the turmoil in my heart, Lord, all my desires are before you, and my sighing is not hidden from you.

—Psalm 38:8-9

How can we all identify with groans? We have all had valleys when we groan in our painful thoughts and overwhelming circumstances, and life with its valleys, and we complain internally, and only the Lord hears our cry.

We who know the Lord know one who intercedes for us, and even though our words cannot be expressed, the Lord knows the secrets of our minds. We smile at each other and hug, yet we cannot say our hearts for many reasons. One might fear someone not understanding or not wanting another with an opinion and a know-it attitude.

We are very blessed if we have that one safe person in our life whom we can be honest with and spill the floods of our soul; that one who loves us and knows our faults and our failures and sees us and remains their friend. This is what Jesus wants to do with us.

Even as believers, we rarely get to this place because we all keep running to the human touch to fix our emotions. We think if we vent and they agree with us, this will remove the hurts of our hearts, and all along, they are listening with their injuries and cannot fill you when they need to be served themselves, so together we share but never resolve the groans of our soul.

We never learn to rise, be still, listen, read the Word, and be honest and authentic with the greatest Friend you will ever need or have.

We become self-sufficient, so we prepare for the day, exercising, putting on our attire, eating the correct foods, and drive off and forget all about the One who allowed you to rise, provided you your food and clothes, and gave you the ability to have a car and to drive and forgot without Him you will not go anywhere but in reverse.

We don't want to wait until we have the groans and agony that fill us to the brink before we learn to praise the Lord who loved you enough that He let his own Son die for you. He let His own Son die just because of love. Love is a word lacking today. Love of self we all know and recognize.

We will go to the extreme with ourselves. Denying self, we don't meet many of those people today, and when we do, we describe them in our self-righteousness as weak or they are too emotional. People around them do not understand that they have sold out to Christ and surrendered to a Lord, and those who are still in the carnal state stand and ask, "why you don't get yourself together" when they stand full of the world and we are in the Lord so a spiritual warfare is declared.

Spiritual warfare is like a brushfire today. We see life out of control for many of our family and friends, and we look to the warnings and the eastern sky. He is coming soon, and this is good news because where some do not have hope for tomorrow, let us let them see the hope in us, and may the groans in us be turned outward to them to teach them this Christ we know that overcomes all cries, hurts, and heals those wounds because that is what He gave his life for. Then maybe we will all learn to turn groans into praise.

Memories Of A Bible School

Little children, I shall be with you a little while longer; you will seek me, and as I said to the Jews, where I am going, you cannot come, so now I say to you a new commandment: I give to you, that you love one another as I have loved you that you will also love one another.

—Luke 13: 33 -34

How can I ever forget the man of God in our little one-room church who came to lead in Bible school? He announced that on one of the days, "Whoever memorizes Psalm 24 will receive this gold ink pin." My heart became so excited because I had never seen a fountain pen like that due to our limited funds growing up.

I remember a deep, strong voice saying the words from the Bible, "Who is this king of glory?" Who may stand in his holy place? *He who has clean hands and a pure heart*, and it stuck forever in my heart and soul.

During this Bible school at eleven or twelve years of age, I remember walking down front and giving my heart to Jesus all because a man took the time to reach us children for the Lord. Ever since that day, I have had painful memories and valleys, yet the Jesus he introduced me to carried me through every valley and resided with me on the mountaintop.

My heart and memories from that little one-room church taught me that Jesus had protected me, loved me, and forgave me, and when I sing "What a Friend I have in Jesus," it is beyond measure the meaning of a friend. I later lost the ink pen, but I never lost Jesus, who lives in me today, and He wrote His words on my heart just like the ink pen did on paper.

He chose a little Kentucky girl, and He can pick you; only be available and want Him and let Him write his words in your heart, and He also will carry you through your valleys and hard times and let this king of glory come into your heart.

My Little One-Room Church

For God so loved the world that that He gave his only begotten Son, that whoever believes in Him should not perish but have everlasting life.

–John 3: 16

I guess you would say that I experienced things before my time. As a little girl, I remember sitting in a one-room church on a pew in a corner, and this was acting as my Sunday School room. We all had places for our ages, and you could hear everybody talk at once, but I could hear the name of JESUS. We would read those Bible verses, and I did not know what they all meant, but I still listened to the word JESUS.

After preaching, we would gather and talk and invite the Preacher home for dinner. This was the middle of the day meal then, and boy, was it dinner. My mom would kill a chicken with her strong arm and fry it golden brown and make bread and pies from a cabinet of a few bought supplies, but when she took that old tablecloth off, a feast was before us like the basket of bread and fishes in the Bible that fed many people.

I remember women in the church giving their testimonies of what Jesus did for them and what he meant to them, and again, I would hear the name JESUS. They called it a "Cry and Testify." I would see them leave their pew and walk over to maybe a relative or brother or sister and would lead them to the Lord and go down with them to lead them into the kingdom.

They cared enough for that person's life, and where they would spend eternity; nobody would get upset or accuse them of a self-righteous attitude; they received it as love of a fellow man and love of a soul for Christ.

I remember Christmas Eve and again in that little one-room church, I would hear the name of JESUS, being born in a stable, and those dear people instilled in us as children things money could not buy or ever be replaced because there was no money to purchase gift and decorate today, only the name of JESUS was shared.

I remember a preacher who never had a salary only because he received a love offering from a people who worked below minimum wage. Still, there was enough there that fed him and us to preach the name of JESUS again. I remember Bible School, taking a cigar box and clothes pins and painting them, and making a doll bed for our baby doll. Then, after playing, I heard the name of JESUS.

One day, Brother Dockery came and impacted my life; I have never been the same since that day. He was teaching us children about JESUS, and this person, JESUS, became real to me, and I accepted HIM along with Brother Dockery's daughter. He challenged us to memorize Psalm 24, and we would receive a gold fountain pen, which was rare when we hardly had a pencil.

I worked hard, and this scripture is embedded in my heart today. And well, I was the winner of that Pen, which I will never forget, and when I heard his deep voice say, WHO IS THE KING OF GLORY? I will never forget how this sounded in my ears. I was a winner in many ways that day; I had scripture engraved in my soul to carry me through some of the deepest waters of my life.

I have memories of that little church where the Aunts and Uncles and the neighborhood people were making footprints on my heart that would carry a message of JESUS with me today. There was a river the Preacher took us to have us baptized, and there was no fear that day. Even though my parents always said not to go in that river, there are deep water step-off places. I knew that Preacher had me by one hand and JESUS by the other, and my fear faded. I came up from the water with little understanding of what was happening to me and where this day would lead me.

I am in a big city now, and nobody takes preachers home for dinner anymore. We sure do not go to the next aisle and talk to someone about their souls; we would probably be ousted from the church. Hearts have changed, and a crust has built around them, so we don't feel for our brother like before. I guess there will not be any more Sunday afternoon tales about the old rabbit that ran from the hound dog and no more family that sticks together like a brother, quilting together on an afternoon while venting our concerns about our life.

We made candy and butter and never heard the word lonely on that day, all because JESUS was heard without all the drowning of noises from Malls, cars, and the lures of Satan leading us away from hearing the name of JESUS.

In all this technology age where we have all money can buy, what that little one-room church gave to me and all the uneducated people around me taught me was the name of JESUS, and money cannot believe this or take this away from me. I see children today, including my own and grandchildren, and ask, am I one of those women in my little one-room church that cares enough to let them know and hear the word JESUS and what he has done for me and praise Him, I wonder?

Our Lost Generation

And the Lord passed before him and proclaimed. The Lord, the Lord God, merciful and gracious, longsuffering and abounding in goodness and truth, keeping mercy for thousands, forgiving iniquity and transgressions and sin by no means clearing the guilty, visiting the enormity of the father upon the children and children's children to all third and fourth generation.

—Exodus 34 6-7

My heart grieves over our children and grandchildren today. In Grandma's day, it was a deep, dark secret where a child was sexually abused, and now we fear sexual predators in our neighborhood or maybe within the confines of our homes.

Watching the media and seeing so many children missing, killed, and abused, I remember His words. *Those who hurt these little ones of mine should have a millstone around their neck* rather than hurt Christ's little children. The children are precious to our Lord.

We have become a society that gets up every morning, looks in the mirror, sees flaws in our bodies and minds, and tries to alter what God has created. The 20-21st-century mother rushes to work, and with all the clothes, her checkbook maybe cannot be able to afford to pay, and then more, she has all the jewelry that drapes from even the navel on her body and a tattoo revealed when she bends.

She feels so inadequate to the bosom because she has seen TV, movies, and books that say if you have an enhancement, you will be noticed and find love and the attention she craves and lacks.

These mothers work until exhaustion, trying to afford what their depleted souls desire. She then opens a can and rushes the little ones to bed and up the following day to start again and never gain the much-needed peace she strives to have. We are a tired bunch of mothers, and our short fuse releases the frustration of our lives. And we raise a generation of children that also runs on empty for that touch, kiss, and hug from their parents that each child deserves.

These generations of parents have created debt that chains them to a routine that does not allow them to parent the children, laugh with them, and grow with them. We are rearing children with much needed attention and behavior learned by parents who are still destitute. They do not have parenting skills because they also have issues they pass on to their children.

These children do not crave what our checkbooks and paydays will buy them; they want us to be still, hold them, love them, and teach them about the ONE who has all their future.

There is a song: people need the Lord, and our grown adult children need a Savior, and when they return to the rock, then their families and future will be full of peace, and they will quit running to every source to fill up the hole inside of them that only Christ can fill.

The 20th-century mother enters her children into ballerinas, sports, cheerleading, and maybe into many church activities. By the time the homework is presented, the family is on edge because of exhaustion and fatigue. It is so simple, mothers, quit spending, quit activities, and hold that one and throw the ball in your yard, tell your children they are unique and love and exercise by example and give them the attention they so crave, or are you still craving attention so bad you cannot see beyond yourself, take a look a the big *I*.

We throw a DVD into a machine or stream something to babysit our little ones. We never examine the words they learn or the message they know, and we wonder why our 120 children misbehave. The family has forgotten that Red Rover and kickball do not cost anything, but time does not.

The 20th/21st-century family has become a selfish generation, and it is all about me; however, the justification is I work and give and buy for them to have a big home and can be in all these things, but have we examined this indeed, is it maybe all about you? The WORD says we labor in vain unless the Lord builds the house. We let another individual raise our children and grandchildren and ask ourselves, what is wrong with this generation?

We should be asking ourselves, what is wrong with me? Am I selfish, self-centered, and like to play with the children and be their friends? But we don't want to parent because it is so hard. We would have to give up our toys and our time for me, so until we face the truth about our life and our motives, we will raise a generation of lost children who never have the name of Jesus mentioned. This generation will be our nation's next leaders; that is scary, though, isn't it?

We pass through this life once with our children, and when we are so selfish that we do not take the time with our children and let money and jobs become our focus and not keep it balanced, it will fulfill the Word of God we reap what we sow.

Are we sowing lasting seeds in our children that will help them to return to a truth you have taught them, or have you yet learned the truth yourself so you can prepare these little ones?

The Word says to train a child in the way he should go, and when he is old, he will not depart; what are we teaching? Work twenty-four seven, make all the money you can so you can buy all the toys, become self-centered, and if there is any time left, then the family will be worked in, no time for God, not even on Sunday; we like to relax because we have had a hard week so we fish, play golf, hunt or just sleep, but *we deserve it* we tell our self and all along Satan is winning the battle all because of self.

We dress the outside while the inside is never attired, and the heart is reflected by our lifestyles, speech, and actions, and people know where we are sowing our seeds. Today's children think they are ugly and don't measure up because the emphasis is on how we look, so relationships are in crisis. They are crying out in pain because they have made wrong decisions after bad decisions. We tried to fix them when we do not even try to fix ourselves and the children stand there learning your behavior.

While watching, they also carry this behavior into their marriage, their homes, and wrong decision after bad decision is made. They wonder why nothing works and why the name of Jesus was never taught nor learned. There is no time for the Lord, but all the time for self trying to fix our broken life and broken dreams because we were never taught and on and on. It goes with the cycle until that one parent steps up to the plate and takes responsibility for their actions and then their children.

The Bible is shelved in homes with dust, and our hearts are never clean all because of our choices with our time and preferences of our decisions for life. We still drink milk that the Word says, not eat the solid food of God's Word. We need to grow up and admit the truth; we have left the one who wants us to come to him, and He will fix all our messes.

Today's adult children are locked up little girls and boys who refuse to grow up and face the fundamental responsibilities of parenthood. If the control of life is lost and we sacrifice ourselves and become last, then the selfish heart is revealed.

This generation is selfish, and we are losing children all because raising children is hard, and we want them, but let somebody else take the hard stuff because it is not cutting into what the big I want to do. The entitled generation is here, and the children's eyes are learning a behavior that says shop and put on clothes and look good with our nails, toes, jewelry, SUV, and have fun and eat out all your meals, so are we raising children who will not know how to cook, spend all their husband's money and let a stranger raise their children, and never eat a meal at grandma's house, because grandma is gone to the cafeteria.

Will our adult children return to God and his house and return to the basics of a home where mother nurtured, dad played and prayed and got the family up to go to church, and jobs all ceased on God's holy day?

Our adult children need to learn wealth comes from knowing Christ and his Word that will carry us through the unexpected curves in life and admit sin is sin. More divorces and a broken home mean more children are confused and more attention deficit being detected, but is it? Is the attention a result of confusion in the lives of their parents and homes?

The schools are seeing a result of parents and their neglect of children and want the educators to fix their problem. The development of the lifestyle raises its ugly head, and all our sins will be found out, and then trying to fix the hole may be too late.

If adult children would learn that when they are tiny and easy to mold, to fill them full of the Lord and pray and take time to understand themselves about God, our future society would know right from wrong, and the value of life would be precious to them.

Are we teaching them sex is for marriage, not to protect themselves from an unwanted child, and are we teaching them to show respect for authority figures, teachers, police, parents, and adults? And do they have the manners to say, "thank you and please?" Little children are acting out their confusion, frustrations, and hurts.

They do not know how to process the adult behavior that is not hidden from their little innocent eyes, so wake up adult parents and see your little child crying in the wilderness for you; it is not what you can buy but you and your time, which is all they seek.

Are you seeking the world to fill up your aches and pains, and there is no room for your children to fix their little hearts and lives? Are you so hungry to love yourself because you do not love yourself, and you are also trying to find a person or things to validate you are loved and of worth?

Why not try Jesus? He is all you need, not a person or something, and move fast toward this because you do not have time to lose your children; catch them before they slip away.

Remarriages, live-ins, gay and homosexual lifestyles, porn websites, and sexual predators—wake up, parents! If you do not give children what they need, these people will, and we may lose them forever to this society; we must have Jesus.

People Running

Do you know that those who run in a race all run, but one receives the prize? Run in such a way that you may obtain it.

—1 Corinthians 9:24

As I watch the turmoil of our world, I see searching people running here and there for a fix, yet it never fills up the hole only Christ can fill. More malls, more buying, less time with family, and the stresses that send us to doctors because of fatigue that engulfs us.

We as a people will not stand still and let the Lord bring to our minds all the garbage that has accumulated in each one of us. We are like the hourglass on the computer; it stands searching because it's so full, and finally and slowly, it lets the page of our life appear.

When it does seem like a mirror to our soul, we don't like what we see. We may see selfishness, we don't like about ourselves, and we may see our self-centeredness around our children, and their hurts are so ingrained that the Lord is their only hope. We may see neglect of a marriage, where we alienated our partner for another life, or maybe a divorce we may have regretted.

We are lazy people, and we don't want to do the hard stuff, like looking at the little girl and little boy in each one of us and acknowledging we remain hurt, neglected and may have an unforgiving spirit that lingers from our past, and this might just be the key to having the abundant life that Christ wants us to have.

As we see a glimpse of ourselves, we may see the neglect of an elderly parent that we were just too busy to help along the way; our selfishness is not the Christ-like walk; it is our flesh that takes over our minds, and if Satan can lure us to surf the net, shop, drive, party and be in our world of busyness, then we will not have time to hear that still small voice what about me?

I gave you the husband and the car, the gas, the clothes, the home and children, and your talent. We try to keep guilt suppressed and out of our lives. It is easy to attend a meeting when we are accepted at work or church on school committees. It fills the fellowship of the loneliness of our souls and makes the time fill up with things that our flesh feels are essential.

Still, when the evening comes and the light of the day then turns to darkness, we run to the remote and fill our minds again with the media that fills us with the noise of all the wars, shootings, and national disasters and lay on our pillow wondering why peace does not prevail. Then we sigh with a thought: this has not been a good day; why?

Most people take a remote and fill their minds with trash, and yet the most excellent book still lays with the dust and new pages never turned that could speak to our hearts and minds and fill us with the enjoyment of Christ and take away the guilt, confusion and give us a peace that only Christ can provide.

If we would but lay down the remote, stop running back and forth like a bird at the seaside, and let our time be spent surfing for spiritual knowledge instead of the world's clamor.

We, as a people, have it all and have nothing. Even saints run and pray, sing and attend meetings, and maybe go out the door and not treat a family member, neighbor, or fellow church member with God's love.

Until we park our cars, lay down the remotes, log off the computers, and let our souls be quiet, only then will we find the peace, joy, happiness, fulfillment, and contentment that drugs, doctors, houses, people, clubs and exercise and cell phone conversations cannot fill the hole of our heart that we are so desperately trying to fill, only Jesus, can you hear me now, only Jesus.

Remember When

Remember your creator in the days of your youth before the
difficult days come and the years draw near when you say I
have no pleasure in them.

—Ecclesiastes 12:1

Do you remember when visiting family was a priority on our grand-parent's day, and there were no malls or shopping on Sunday? We went to church and maybe even invited the preacher to lunch. Parents worked hard physically, Monday through Friday, polishing shoes to go to town on Saturday, but when we came to Sunday, you knew it was a special day.

If a lost soul was there, you might have one of the Godly saints reach across the aisle and lead that soul to the Kingdom. There was time; there was love and feeling for a brother. If a baby was born, women in the community went; if a house burned, they helped to build it back; if a crop failed, they shared with their fellow neighbors, and when the harvest was ready, men came together to pool their labor for each other.

Women visited in the afternoons with children, and children played with the only things of nature, maybe a bloom from a flower that was like an egg, or maybe a tin can was a cup, and a stick was a fork used things thrown away to reach the imagination of the minds. Toys? What was that? Maybe a secondhand tricycle, but we all were the same, poor maybe in our eyes, but oh so rich.

Cars were rare, phones were scarce, and loaf bread and biscuits were still used in lunch boxes all around. The dinners were cooked by a loving mother who wanted to love her children and feed them the labor of her love. Flour and water, potatoes, and beans were used in many ways that always created something new for us children. I think of the loaves of bread and the fish in his Word, where after they there was more than enough and yet had some left, and Mother could take nothing and have a feast.

There was no cooking channels, no Dr. Phil, no doctors in reach, no grocery chains, only a few good men who, when somebody was hungry or sick, circled around you and cared enough to give the sacrifices of their own resources, and also had children to feed and lacked prosperity, but they had love.

Women shared their hearts and were not afraid of being real and honest; they did not have antidepressants and pills. They accepted their bodies and faced what God gave to them without makeover because they discovered it was the beauty inside, not outside, that God wanted.

Their lives stayed busy caring for the home, children and spouses. They built the fires, heated the water to do the laundry, starched the shirts, and ironed from morning till dusk to finish the day's chores. There was no electricity or anything, yet fatigue was not an option; working and leaving children was not an option, but I had time and took time for the important things of life.

A local grocer would trust the community's men and write down each item charged before charge cards were a vision. The loyalty they provided was known by all in the community. Candy behind a glass was a dream; drinks in a cooler were off limits because there was not an extra nickel so

I watched, and then when an uncle or grandfather gave me a penny, I got some candy kisses, and my heart raced with excitement and joy.

I took my time taking off the wrapper and savoring the taste that will never be tasted like that ever again. When the nail kegs, flour sacks, scales so large you could weigh a cow, detergent with dishes, and grass sacks of feed, we took them home, and the excitement filled my heart.

The beautiful dishes my mother would set out on our table, the flour sack she made me a garment of that I wore proudly. Remember the big Brogan shoes that I hated all because our grocer had them and could charge them, and daddy went off on Monday to saw the logs at the sawmill so he could pay the bill next week?

We were taught not to ask for anything that cost money and taught when sitting on a nail keg to rise up when older adults came in and offered our seats. To say *thank you* when a gift of candy was given and it was appreciated is a thing our society has lost. I remember wondering why and how Santa Claus always brought fruit and mom's nylon hose hanging from the mantel, and it stretched to the floor with fruit and nuts.

The smell of a cedar tree roamed the house, and a roaring fire that a parent provided so we would be warm when we awoke. We were prepared to know fruit and nuts may be our only thing Christmas morning, but we did not know what a Christmas list was anyway, so we had love, which was a gift.

Attending a one-room schoolhouse, crank telephones, oil lights or kerosene lights, wash pots, and seeing the 20th-century children walk into a marriage today, buying a home, and furnishing it with all the gadgets, I stand in awe.

I hear their cries of depression, unhappiness, escaping with alcohol and drugs and I think about those days of each of us staying in tune with needs of the community, sharing our food and caring for the sick and wonder with all the money that materialism can buy, but this generation searches for something to fill up the emptiness that cannot be filled and they will never know that stopping, being still and sharing their hearts, time and love would remove all the crutches they use to remove the pain in their hearts.

Houses, not homes, children with part-time parents, schools with guns and not fist fights, sex instead of purity, and TV and videos and not a church, malls and not visiting, caring hearts instead of the BIG I, sacrifices instead of selfishness, washing feet instead of walking on feet, heal a heart, not break a heart, girls dressing modestly not wearing a suggestive wardrobe, a child to be child not endure adult roles, a blush instead of no conscience.

We have moved from poor with the richness of life to the richness and loss of the meaning of life. Young adults think of being on a golf course, having nails done, hair salons, body sculpting, tanning, spas, body trainers, and surgery reconstructing a body the Lord gave us for our own DNA and identity.

We go to malls to clothe our aching hearts with fashion that covers the outside, but the inside is still null and void. We are a confused society and we wonder why girls have been married two and three times or have live ins, abortions and all on the rise, all because when the woman forgot her way and Satan lured her away from the home and he knew if he could destroy the home and family, he would be on his way.

When daycare started parenting our children, not the parents' parents began to give more to their children and more than the generation before them. VCR, DVD, Internet, and now iPods have become a lifestyle for our now children and grandchildren, and this has become a chat room for our children and grandchildren. Then the minds are filtered with violence, sex, and another avenue for Satan to lure children and parents don't hear the sounds of their children crying out for someone to chat with them, and a stranger takes the time, not a mom and dad.

Our church pews are empty because we say to ourselves, we have freedom, it's my life and my body I will do what self wants to do, and yet never enter the Word of God that says to us all, there are rules, and when you break my rules, you are heading in the wrong direction.

As parents and grandparents, do we sit idle and say nothing, or do we live life before them and mention the name of Jesus so somewhere when they enter society, they will have heard the name Jesus can we help stop this runaway generation that is so desensitized to the name of Jesus all because we have not told them or just maybe they might turn around and look at us and say, well what about you?

Maybe just one of us can make a difference, well what about you?

The Circle Around Me

For He shall be like a tree planted by the water, which spreads out its roots and will not fear when heat comes, but the leaf will be green, and will not be anxious in the year of the drought nor will cease from yielding fruit.

—Jeremiah 17:8

A circle around me, a challenge for me, faces me today. "I Shall Not Be Moved" has become not a song but a statement in the core of my being. I ask you, Lord, when I am not the one with the morality in question, why do I have a circle of female family and extended family circling me? What are you teaching me, I ask?

Is my heart not pure? Is it my attitude? Is it my thoughts, Lord? What I ask are you teaching my soul? My flesh says I don't feel like loving and forgiving and seeking. Without you, Jesus, in my being, I would not even question my decision, but when you went to the old rugged cross, you died for me, you suffered, you were humiliated, and you were scorned and shamed, but love overcame it all, so are you teaching me again how to love?

My hurts, my disappointments, my aches keep me from a phone, save me from the right words, and I ask for mercy and grace and your power over my weakness, your control over my broken heart, your authority over all the sins inside me, so Lord I cannot overcome in my strength. You made the blind to see, you parted the Red Sea, now Lord help me to love and forgive.

142

What Happened To Family

Surely you have things turned around; shall the potter be esteemed as the clay, for shall the thing make say of him who made it he did not make me? Or shall the thing formed say of him who formed it, he has no understanding?

—Isaiah 29:16

In our younger years, we had families and reunions, played with cousins in fields, and let the child in us be free to be a child. Did we ever think one day reunions would not be had and families would be so mixed up with his, hers, and theirs that we would not know what family reunion we are attending?

One by one, a family member is taken to glory, and in the blink of an eye, we are the seniors, and our children and grandchildren are looking to us as the older generation, and now we are in line. There are faces of sadness all around ones who have lost their spouse; no words can fix their hearts. We must learn to trust the only One who can mend our hearts and lives.

We must take our remaining days and live for a Christ who owns it all and loans us the children and grandchildren as a gift for us to enjoy as we travel this road called life. Families with burdens, yet do they learn to lean on the Everlasting Arm? Jesus is the comfort; He searches every crevice of our hearts, and like clay, He does not stop molding us. And He keeps putting us in His hands and setting us close.

We move away, and then He grabs us and molds us again because it is painful, and we run from pain. We don't want it His way; we want it our way, and we want to tell the potter how to mold our clay, but Christ wants us to lay still and let Him have His way and let Him set us, and if we will be still and know this Savior we will fulfill his purpose and plan of our life.

Christianity is not a part-time job; it requires daily working, giving, loving, and forgiving, so why do we not begin our day taking up our cross so we will face our remaining years full of joy and completeness? God will become sweeter daily; then, we will learn to praise him and feel that peace we have never known. Let the potter have the wheel and be still, and let him mold you into a new creature.

Where Is Love?

But I say to you who hear: Love your enemies, do good to those who hate you, bless those who curse you, and pray for those who spitefully use you.

—Luke 6:12

Where is your love? Is it all for you and none for me? Do you, after you finish with you, have any left? Today, as we look around, these are the words of our generation of children, every hearing of abuse, no respect for life, stealing what is not theirs, and this is a world away from God and is an infiltration of our children and grandchildren.

We must take responsibility, and just because we put them in homes other than our own, we expect others to teach them respect, love, and discipline from strangers, and so goes the world. As we watch our children and grandchildren, we know times have changed, and hearts are further away from the Lord than the generation before us.

Using plastic and spending an income not yet there and many homes with blended families and live-ins all around, children are hurting. We watch the thirty-year-olds and up and realize they are still needy and searching for a way to bring relief to a pressured world where they have made choices.

They seek toys, other mates, a job, and minds so divided that wrong choices are made because of emotions that are so needy that sometimes there is no return to those choices that were made with compulsion.

They try to cope in a world of messages of a false sense of security, and when this does not work, they take a drink, take a drug, and maybe they can escape the pressures of life all because nobody told them Christ is the coping tool for their life.

Young adults need to be held and need reassurance so badly of their worth. They produce children, and because of their neediness, they look up and say, hey, what about me? I need to be reassured, I need to be hugged, I need, I need, I need, but you are so busy with self you fail to see the signals of your children.

Children are crying out, saying, "I need you to love me, hold me; I need to know you love me above your hobby, your job, your wife, your husband; I need to know the world is not loved by you more." They are screaming to know you can be counted on and be there when they need help instead of hurrying home, opening a can, taking a bath, putting them to bed, and calling that spending time.

A video has become your babysitter and fills the minds of children with fears and aggression, with a taught behavior that they learn to handle conflict violently because you never monitored and edited the activities of their day and time.

When they begin to act out a behavior, we ask what we will do with them all along because of the liberal thinking and never measuring the activities of your home with the Word of God. An alarm goes off that there may be a problem, and never accept the responsibility as a parent of the example you set before those little hearts and minds.

Children are crying out for your love and attention; if you do not fill them now, there will be an individual later that will, and it will not be your choice. We then lose control of their world and see they, just like us, are trying to fill up the empty hole that never gave them the security, reassurance, and love that they cried out for in their homes and when marriages are tried out in multiple times, will the name of Jesus ever be uttered and will they know enough to return to Him or know enough of Him.

If adult parents do not attend church and hear, how can they teach the children when they do not have enough to survive life's storms? How do we reach a hurting generation of little children? We need to get our adult parents first, and it may trickle into the hearts and minds of children and grandchildren.

A routine for many is to work hard all week to provide money for a home and do chores on Saturdays. Sunday is a day of rest so that I will sleep and lounge so I can face next week, and on and on it goes. I never hear the name Jesus, and the children think Sunday is a day of fun with the parents to go and shop or take a one-day trip all along, and the children never hear JESUS.

We reap what we sow, which is hard enough in a world where sin is not felt anymore.

There is no conviction, so we must quit loving ourselves, turn the football game off, stop shopping to kill time, and find jobs for a forty-hour week. Maybe this will leave time for you to hug them, reassure them that you are there, and fill the children's lives with security that no person or gift bought can replace the security of a parent.

When our focus is in a mirror, and it is all about me, the children live a pattern of what is acted out before them so that they may exercise, may shop, may try to fill up their holes, but when your child is in a spot with you, what then? Grow up, quit drinking a bottle of milk, eat the meat like Christ told us to do, and invest time with Christ and your children;

then, it may not be happily ever after, but you will have invested in the hereafter.

Part Four

God's Creation

Dear Reader,

Unlike any of God's creations, the ocean has intrigued me with its beauty and power. I focus my writings on the shoreline of His pulsating rhythmic waves, washing in the hope and out the sins and mistakes of my life. I feel the peace and incredible fear that His water and wind can wreak on humanity. His power is ultimate, and my spirit is humbled each time I visit the power of His creations.

For some of you, experiencing the ocean might be your dream; for others, your awe might stand in the height of His Mountains, rivers, deserts, forests, or plains. The point and boldness of this section is to share my testimony that His creations feed our souls and confirm His glory and Majesty.

God doesn't shout or scream at us. He loves us and will demonstrate His power in the waves and winds of a storm. Those moments are for us to turn and praise and pray. His hand gathered the elements that shaped and formed our very life, the planet on which we could physically dwell and spiritually find Him daily.

In this section, you will see my worship and praise of my God as I sit in humble awe and wonder at His power and life-sustaining energy He blesses all of us with—no matter our actions. He still provides nature and wonders to our souls in the hopes that we will feel joy and happiness, and in that state of love, we will turn and return to Him.

At The Seaside

My grace is sufficient to you, for my power is made perfect in your weakness.

—2 Corinthians 12:9

As the waves roar and I see the sun with all its rays, it reminds me of your power. You said in Genesis that you created light to separate the sea from land. When you started the wonders of it all, I stand in amazement at even the birth of a human and nothing we have done in our strength for that creation.

How the hands and each part are so detailed, and as I see what a vast ocean lays before me, your love of man is much greater. You control the sunrise, the tide, and the times of all nature, so how can we ever doubt the timing of each person in our life and the time of a day when circumstances do not catch you off guard?

Each person is not a surprise, yet we allow the struggles and pain to take our focus off you when you want us to take the pain and struggle, learn who you are, and trust you. Our hearts and minds must be renewed by your word daily so that when we take up the cross, we are obedient and focus on your power and strength, not the burden and mountains we cannot overcome.

Satan seems to know our weaknesses and takes the things most precious to us. We can either fall on our knees because the Lord wants us to come to him, trusting him to see our reaction, and wants our hearts to trust. We must be still and know he is god. He will always be an on-time God.

Remember Abraham with Isaac and in obedience with his hand drawn back, and he knew God would provide the lamb or his son to be brought back from death, yet he was obedient. Just trust me is His message; His thoughts are not my thoughts; His ways are not mine, says the Lord.

God is still on the throne, watching and waiting, so Lord, help us today to trust in the Holy God, and if He had the power to create this ocean and the vastness beyond man, we would trust in Holy God in a world-changing every day.

He is always there and will not leave us nor forsake us today or tomorrow; He is the great I Am today and always.

Comparison Of An Ocean

Praise the Lord from the earth, your great sea creatures and all ocean depths.

—Psalm 148:7

The vastness and power of the roar of the ocean waves reveal what an awesome god we serve. The beauty of an ocean, a sunrise, and a moon over nature has been given for our enjoyment and rest.

We take these gifts for granted and never go beyond our selfishness to realize who gave them and all who created this vastness of what we see. We are like the sandpiper with our heads in the sand, thinking of what we are getting out of it all and what to fulfill.

When we truly listen and are still and know a god and hear a god and see a god, only then will we see the ocean, the sun, and the moon from His perspective, not man. When again circumstances all around look out of control, but if he controls a high and low tide, sunset and moon to rise, how much more will he handle the circumstances of our life? Every life must have cases to draw us to a god of love.

When this doesn't draw, then he gives one more chance and one more and one more. Some people never yield nor give up their fleshly control, so they go to the doctor for a pill, a therapist to tell their woes, or to a friend who is worse off than them and maybe drown in drugs or alcohol.

It grieves our lord to see a life wasted because of the stubborn and callous heart and never to turn to him who gives peace, tranquility, and a friend who sticks closer than a brother. When a man makes decisions based on their emotions and flesh, then he will most likely take the wrong road.

Man can be highly educated and wealthy beyond measure, but if the lord is missing in this journey called life, then all will never give the security they are looking for. Enough is never enough, plenty is not plenty, and just like the ocean waves, they go back and forth, coming forward for a while and finally going out again and never gaining ground.

Only when the storm comes, and the uncertainty begins, so is our life. When the winds blow, we will see if our houses are built on a firm foundation and stand firm on pillars like steel, or will your wind blow down a lifetime of planning and building and leave all desolate without hope?

Will we turn in our humility, revert to anger and disobedience, begin to build in our strength, and never turn to a most excellent builder who has the blueprints and survey our soul? Some always need to learn who the builder is; their plans and dreams are shambles.

The American dream has been lost all because sin has become a way of life and the conscience seared, and that little voice that once convicted us has let the flame grow dim just like the sandpiper heads still in the sand searching only for their gain.

We must pull our heads out of the sand and put away the drugs and drinks and activities that numb the mind and soul and begin to hear the one calling from this beautiful creation given to us as an example and for us to enjoy and maybe like the stillness of a sunset and the day is finished we will return to the one who is the creator of all creations.

Creation Our Teacher

In the beginning, God created the heaven and the earth.

— Genesis 1:1

Words cannot express the beauty of a sunset or the roar of an ocean's wave. Do I think I am here by chance? No, it is all the Gods of creation providing the means and revenue of every gift that enables me to release all the pressures of this life and the tension I hold on to.

I am reminded again of the God who knows when the sun begins to rise and high tide and the moon that disappears with the light of day. Furthermore, He knows when I wake and breathe and controls every hair that falls from my head, so why do I seem to hold on to the burdens, and why don't I focus on the one who had a plan even in my mother's womb?

He brought me thus far, and he will get all those we love through the valleys and paths he has for each of them. As I cannot control the force of the waves, neither can I manage time and circumstances, so help me, Lord, as I learn again to release, repent, and trust.

May you bring me closer to the life of freedom like the gulls who soar above my head and help me also to soar and let you lift me higher, feel your presence under mywings, and let me fly.

Emotions Rolling Like The Waves

Then God's peace, which goes beyond anything we can imagine, will guard your thoughts and emotions through Christ Jesus.

—Philippians 4:7

Emotions roll like the waves of an ocean, back and forth and taking us to places maybe beyond return, but we know a God who knows it all and every grain of sand and every wave of an ocean and is in his control.

He created it and every creature, so how much more does he know me and cares about us? The sand rubs, and it hurts if we let it rub and never put an ointment on the rub. Christ wants to be our ointment to our sores that hurt us, but when we apply the balm ourselves, and we say we do not need his help, we will do it ourselves, then we hurt and hurt, the rub leaves a scar for life, and all we ever learn is don't let the sand rub you.

You may not know what God wants to teach you when the Lord wants to search our hearts and souls. He will make the rub hurt more next time until we are ready to listen. He is the great physician who heals all our rubs of this life, and the waves will take us out, and when we do not grab the lifebuoy that God throws, He will let us either float or drown; it is our choice. We must feed our souls, which is his word, his way, not ours, or we will meet him one day, and all the videos of our life will be played, and we cannot block or blame on that day.

He loves us with a love beyond what man cannot give us. We must take the life preserver and swim back to shore because on that shore are our children and our children's children waiting and confused.

We must give them hope and a life lived before them so they will choose a Jesus, not what all the world offers. Without hope in Jesus, we are all void and will never be filled with whatever we seek. The void is Jesus all because God has his son because of love, so right now, as I look at the ocean, it cannot be measured how wide or deep; that is God's love for us.

Before we let the sand of our life rub us raw and leave a scar, we must learn what God is teaching us, and may we realize and look at his word because man cannot give us a plan for our life.

If we were going on a journey, we would get out our map, chart the way, and ask ourselves, how am I going? This would prevent us from getting lost, and we all arrive at our destination.

The destination for us that Christ wants is all of us to follow his map, which is his word. When we start driving our own lives and never taking out the word, we will all come to a dead-end street and never find our way. We must take out a map of God, let him chart our course, and he will never lead us to detours.

Jesus loves us as big as this ocean; He does not care about everything we think is essential. May the sand of our lives not rub us too deeply because Christ stands at the shore, wanting and waiting for us all to not drift too far from him and let him be our healer.

Escaping

Like a bird that wanders from its nest is a man who wanders
from his place.

—Proverbs 27:8

Like the birds, people go to and fro at the sea, but unlike the birds, they have a soul. The people walk, run, and laugh, and we all try to escape the pressures of this life and become like children but return as adults with still old behaviors.

The roar of an ocean and the sun glistening on the waves makes us all feel a sense of peace and release. We think stopping in our souls of all the world's clamor and seem to lose the hold that life sometimes puts on our minds and souls. We walk, talk, fish, swim, and play unlike any other time, and then we ask why I can't feel this freedom when I return to the reality of this world.

A closer revelation of a God of creation and realizing who gave it all and how small I am fills my mind. God is so big that he separated the land from the sea, day from darkness, and so much water, yet a drought and heat like no other time leave our minds boggled trying to understand it all. We may be able to control some things in our lives, but we will never be able to handle this awesome God of all creation.

How Can You Not Believe

I do believe help me in my unbelief.

—Mark 9:24

How can a man look at an ocean, see the sunrise, and not believe in you, Lord? How do they rise and know their breath is allowed one more day? The beauty of the eastern sky throws the rays and sun peeping its head at the water's edge. How can man not believe?

When the sun knows the exact time to rise and see all the power, I am reminded of your word to watch the Eastern sky. When the rays spread across the sky, we glimpse you, which is only a little of what it will be like.

Help us, Lord, to be ready to watch and ensure our hearts are clean and that all your power and love are us. Can we be prepared for your magnificent return?

Katrina, The Message From The Lord

And he sees the sword coming against the land and blows the trumpet to warn the people.

—Ezekiel 33:3

As I sit today looking at the ocean's waves and watching TV, I hear the sounds of your warnings, Lord. Can America hear and can they see, and can they feel you now, Lord? All people everywhere now have your attention, but as of 9/11, will we?

When it is over, go on with our lives and forget your warning against the desperation we are reminded of; the food, the air, and the modern conveniences can be taken away very quickly when we cannot pull the fast world we live in for a quick fix.

The frustration and anger begin to surface. We go into a blame game when we all make choices about what we feel and how we react when we are hungry and thirsty. We all go into survival mode, and our faith is tested. I heard an elected official say remember our scripture: when you give to the thirsty, feed the hungry, and cloth the poor, you do unto me, says the Lord. He was angry because people were dying, and we were slow in America to respond.

Lord, help me love my fellow man and less of me and more of you and see and hear and feel like you, Lord, and maybe the compassion and mercy of my soul will be an action, not an effort. I want to live a life that when I walk through the gates of heaven, you will say, well done, thy good and faithful servant. I ask forgiveness today because I do not feel I am there yet, Lord.

Our Own Time, Lord

How precious also are your thoughts to me, o God! If I should count them, they would be more in number than the sand, when I awake, I am still with you.

—Psalm 139:17

Waiting for the sun to rise at the beach and for it to come up at the right moment is such an incredible moment. The morning's colors and the sun's attempt to peep its head from the edge of the earth show us how on time our Lord is.

He makes each wave of an ocean obey the light that appears. We take all for granted to our own time, Lord.

As the spot where the sun rises gets a red glow, it reminds me of what the Lord told us to do and watch the eastern sky for my appearance, and his time draws near. I watch and wait in awe of the beauty of the glow across the water, which gives off a reflection, and like our life, it also gives a thought to others. It may be a good or bad reflection, but we give off one or the other.

I hope today people see a glow and beauty in me and, like the beauty of the sunrise and glow on the water, let my life be something of the beauty of the Lord and His creation in me today.

The Power Of A Storm

See, the storm of the Lord will burst out in wrath, a whirlwind swirling down on the head of the wicked. The Lord's anger burst out like a storm.

—Jeremiah 23:19

Ophelia is a hurricane, and instead of running, we face it with the faith of the media that it will only be a category one. We know it is coming but don't know exactly what it will become.

This is like our life. We know that there are storms in our lives, yet we must not run but stand still and face the consequences; however, most of us run. Our life is like a wave of force when an unexpected problem hits us, whether death, divorce, health problems, job loss, or losses of any kind.

We quickly try to cover our pain when shock and emotion come flooding our souls; we cry and talk by phone and never go to the throne. We quickly realize friends cannot reach the depth of the soul where the pain lies, and like the core of a boil, only Christ can remove the body and have the healing ointment that the open wound needs. We try to put our cream on and put the band-aid on our wound, and then it happens repeatedly. We lose the band-aid frequently, and the hurts are still there. Nobody can fix the damage that only Jesus can heal.

Man is arrogant and stubborn, and if we keep it to ourselves, we can run and play and pretend the hurt is not there when all around us know.

We are like wounded animals, and when that someone gets too close for us to love or care about us, we pull back from that love offered, afraid again of getting our sore scratched, so we refuse the love shown.

Most of us are so hungry for love that we seek it through wrong choices and impulsive decisions that can cost us for the rest of our lives. We think man can fill all the wrongs and never be told about the one relationship that will never change or hurt us and will last for eternity, and his name is Jesus. We quickly realize after wrong decisions that two sick people cannot make each other well.

When, as a child, our needs were never met, we, as little girls and little boys, grow into adulthood but never arrive at the place of adults. We get stuck in the little boy and girl and stay selfish and want our way and act our behaviors in many ways to draw attention to our needy life.

The infected sore grows and grows into infection and spills over to the person trying to love us, and the sore keeps staying open and never healing. We go round and round with our hidden emotions, thinking no one notices, when our behavior reveals our needs all along.

Man cannot fix sin. We think if we ignore the word sin, then we can live without Jesus, and we take our flesh and ignore the Word of God, but we quickly learn it is all in vain. The Bible is your roadmap, like when you take a trip, and you are taking a journey through life. It is there to protect you from the wrong road and direction and reach your destination.

When we make choices on the narrow and wide road, our flesh wants to go the broad route, and we run into a dead-end street. We look around and say to our souls, now what? That open wound now has no band aid, the sore is infected very badly by sin, and the pain is so intense that there is nothing we can do in our flesh works; then do we call on Jesus for help?

This is where he wants you when you run out of all our fixes, face the pain and agony, and ask him to remove the sore and make you well. When we were children, we had to take shots to prevent diseases that would harm us, so it is will the Lord; he wants to remove the infection and heal, and it will hurt many times, and pain will come, and he is the physician who operates on your body and soul, but we must not run.

We must be still, feel the pain, trust him, and let him fix the hurts, and like taking a prescription, we must follow the instructions. When they say take twice a day, we do not take three times a day, just like the word, when he says do not, then don't do it.

We have all watched the floods in New Orleans, and we see a warning from the Lord of what is still coming for us all. We are living our life, and all of a sudden, an unexpected event comes, and we are not prepared, and this is the way it will be at his coming like a thief in the night. We see people on rooftops screaming for help to save them, and this may be how your life will be at the end. Will Jesus pass you on, and you see the boat and will not be allowed to jump in and be saved when it is too late?

We are watching the waves of Ophelia, and they are getting larger and larger, just like life; those waves can take us out in the blink of any eye, and that is why every day, we must prepare for the storm and read the roadmap as we travel this life and then when the unexpected come. Will we be ready?

The Rub Of Life

A person who is depressed is like taking off a person's clothes
on a cold day or like rubbing salt into a wound.

—Proverbs 25:20

When I lie in the sand and feel the rub, I think of life and how it also rubs us to rawness, and only the Lord has an ointment of healing that nothing or no one can heal. Sometimes, our life overwhelms us like a rushing wave, unexpected, and we are knocked down and another hit, and we try in our strength the best we can to get up; little by little, we feel the burn and agitation, and we then begin to access ourselves and feel all the emotion of what happened.

We walk out of the water. Isn't this just like life? When we get our senses, we then access the pain and feel all the emotions of what happened; we feel the warmth of the sunshine in our souls, which is the Holy Spirit-stirring us to a new level of living. We have been taken to deep water to create a new depth of living and god in his mercy, working into us a clean heart and to know him and all his power and glory.

I watch the little bird at sea running so fast and always keeping ahead of the waves and running from what could be a problem we all face, always running from the pain that could hit us, just like one of the ocean's waves. Over and then, we would face the pain that would entrap us or drag us back and forth like the ocean of life that overwhelms us many times.

The birds seem to run so fast and never go anywhere in particular; however, God has provided their nest, and they don't even know the Creator. The trust that the food will be available, and where do they go without the trees? Yet, he knew when he created a vast ocean where each bird would be and where they would go, and so it is with us.

Sometimes, we all run and become so exhausted that we fly away and never accomplish what God created us for. Are we like the little birds, or do we feel his blessings and all his mercy and grace and will be like all the little birds running until we go missing and people will not miss us when we're gone? Did we matter in this life? We need to ask ourselves this question, and then we will find out why we are here.

The Sun, Our Example

The sun rises, and the sun sets and hurries back to where it
rises.

—Ecclesiastes 1:5

As we wait for a sun to rise, our mind races to watch the Eastern Sky. As stated in your words, we watch the rising of the sun's rays slowly; we also know you are waiting on us today as we rise to let our light shine in our lives' darkness.

God reveals his power of allowing us to face a new day and the sun to rise again, the ocean to reflect our power in a tide, and the full moon glow that glistens on the sea shore.

How can we view this glory and not believe in a God of creation? A bird that can swoop down and feed upon the fish to survive and how it is there in the vastness of a sea and only a God can prove in such a time of need. If He takes care of the bird's needs and provides the right time for them, how much more He offers me?

We get caught up in all the materialism and rat race of life, and as we become still, only then do we ponder what an awesome God we serve. As the ocean pulls and tugs at the waves and draws, the Lord in our spirit draws us, drawing, pulling, and we have the lows and highs also just like the tide, so today, as all begin again all new, help us lord to hold to the lifeline of your love and care and help us like the sun that has risen, shine among all we meet.

The Waves Of Life

He stilled the storm to a whisper, the waves of the sea were
hushed.

—Psalm 107:29

As I sit looking at the ocean, how comprehensive and precise each wave is, and the power of the roar, I also see a mighty Lord that knows each sunrise, sunset, and wave. He created a high and low tide that we just watch, yet in our finite understanding, we cannot explain.

When I sometimes air the burdens of my heart with my fellow man, I become aware that man cannot do a thing only listen, and then I begin to see a creator of this ocean, every grain of sand, every creation and shell. Then I realize he is the one I turn to for the understanding and comfort my soul yearns for, and my broken spirit needs a healing touch from the Master's hand.

Suppose the God of the ocean, the God of the sunrise and wind, and each grain of sand can be controlled by Him. In that case, I became aware he can handle every detail of my life, so Lord, here we depend upon you, not man, for all our needs and asking you to rest from the burdens that grieve us so profoundly.

A God who parted the Red Sea, and as I look at the sea before me, I try to comprehend what a high wall all there must have been and how your children, in faith, walked through on dry land and had faith enough the wall of water would not come down on them. We come to you also in our faith, walking through with you, Lord, trusting you with all the burdens, and as we see an impossibility, you know a way on dry ground, and all we see is the water on each side.

Lord, make us a path and create more faith so we may turn every detail over to you. How can we ever doubt so great a God who made an ocean so wide, deep, and powerful? That is the love you have for all of us, so Lord, we praise you for the rest and remove from us the thoughts from our minds that would create any doubts and fill our minds with joy and hope and make in us a mind that we may reflect you and your love for us.

Don't let our life be like the ocean waves that go back and forth and back and forth and never show progress in our life. Help us like an oyster where the sand has rubbed and rubbed and the irritation of life is creating in each one a beauty in your eye, and then when, like the oyster surfaces, you made us a beautiful pearl.

Lord, we all want to be a beautiful pearl, but the pain, irritation, and rubbing must be allowed, and then we will have a life you have created. Then maybe we will be found in someone's life to help them find a God of all this beautiful creation just like us, and through the waves of our life, then like the sand in the oyster, you know what it took to be an oyster and now help us to radiate the beauty of your love and all of your creation.

Too Big To Understand

**Here is the sea, vast and spacious, teeming with creatures
beyond number, living both large and small.**

—Psalm 104:25

The ocean is so deep, vast, and full of creation beyond man's imagination. The grains of sand so rightly placed and the sun knowing when to rise, and here I stand, a person so little, and yet God loves me more than all this. He loves us so much that he gave His only Son for me not to perish.

We sometimes forget he gave us all this beauty of an ocean and seeing the birds flying back and forth, and He knows when one falls, He cares that much. He knew us in our mother's womb and counted every hair on our head daily. How much does anybody know me more than this, not husbands, not friends, nor family?

When I stand at the ocean's edge, I am amazed God can find me and know me, yet He lives in me all the time. The Holy Spirit leads us and molds us to make us into His image, not the image of this world. The roar of an ocean wave, I think of when He calmed the sea; how much more can He calm me? I praise him for all this beauty and His love, His power. I cannot understand how much He loves *little ole me* in the vastness of a seaside.

As I hear the warnings of a riptide, I also hear the warnings that He will be here soon, and we must follow his plan for us. We cannot conquer the ocean, so it is with our life we must depend on the one who has all of us and creation in His hand, and we must share our knowledge and wisdom.

He has blessed us so much with this ocean and all the beauty of the sun and moon; My God is awesome.

Part Five

Society In America

Dear Readers,

It was a typical quiet Tuesday morning in late Summer. The kids had returned to school, the heat was turning down a few degrees, and you began anticipating fall preparation. That morning, you and many of your fellow Americans were mulling about their morning when suddenly, in the eyes of a camera and through the TV screen, you witnessed an airplane tear through the Twin Towers in New York City.

Metal, speed, and extra fuel rip a fireball explosion at the 93-99 floor, sending a shock wave that rippled through America. The people on the plane were gone. The people on those floors were gone. We watched as smoke spiraled upward, and our minds raced to figure out how an accident like this could have occurred.

The accident is tragic, and our hearts race to find peace when, eighteen minutes later, out of the corner of our TV screens, we see a second plane smash a significantly larger giant hole through the south tower. This bomb-like explosion hits America's awareness that this was no accident—a planned attack.

Suddenly, you feel your safety and security footing in a beautiful country be yanked out from under you. As more tragedies struck the day, the emotional tsunami of shock, panic, and fear crashed into you.

You dropped to your knees to pray. Pray for the terror to stop. Pray for the country to heal from the wound bleeding our nation's morality. This is what I felt when 9/11 happened.

The tragedy of that day is not the sole focus of this section, but it was a wake-up call for me, and I thought for America. I have reflected on this day repeatedly and felt that this was a mini peak into how Christ would return—in shocking awe on a quiet and typical Tuesday morning.

During that day of terror, I realized that the society of America has brilliance and brutality. We saw the spectrum of Good and Evil on that day physically play out for all of us to witness. Why? Was it only to prepare us for His Second Coming, or was it to jolt American Society in a jarring manner so that we would kneel, bow our heads, and repent of all the shameful, lustful, and selfish ways? It's possible—I hoped we would turn away from our selfishness and look up toward Him.

America is still a place of freedom, liberty, safety, love, peace, and hope. It is the only place on earth where laws protect our God-given Rights, and yet...we, as a society, are the ones slapping and spitting in God's face. He won't tolerate it for long.

My witness and psalm in writing these chapters were to shout out the immorality that has happened in our free society and that people are choosing openly and blatantly to abandon God's promised land in exchange for feeding our selfishness like Esau sold his birthright for pottage—for himself. I pray we all wake up and turn our ways to the Lord.

America Is The Beautiful

Has a nation ever changed to God? Yet they are not Gods at all, but my people have exchanged their glorious God for worthless idols.

—Jeremiah 2:11

On September 11, 2001, life in the United States changed forever. As we watched on our TV, we could not believe what we were seeing as the WORLD TRADE CENTER was hit by airplanes of our enemy and began tumbling down with hundreds trapped inside. I began to see Christ in His glory and His return that will be like that one day, totally unexpected, and I wonder while I watch and wonder about all those people's salvation.

We in America are all spoiled to the good life, and we have been doing our agenda and being the captain of our own ships. We look at God and say later, "God, we have places to go and things to do, and we will work you into our life when we have time and will work you someday in my schedule."

Our God is jealous, and we in America have been more interested in Wall Street than in God. When reading the Old Testament, we read of how God was fed up with man, and He warned nations and tried to turn them around, but because of sin and their stubborn hearts, they carried on their own will.

We in our churches examine our lives and ask ourselves what is essential. All our lives have been affected, and the pain in our nation is great. We went from the Ten Commandments and prayer in our school being an issue to our statesman and president praying and asking nations to pray.

What happened was that we ran out of resources, and we are supposed to be one nation under God, or are we? The morality of a country has a familiar look like Sodom and Gomorrah, but God is still God. As a nation, we have wealth, technology, and all the wisdom this nation has never known, but it will never replace the God of this nation, the one who owns it all.

Our hearts are sad today and complete, and we see the hand of God working in and through every nation. We have a praying president today and hearing a little nation of Israel, which is God's own, and we realize this hate is because of Jesus. We are fulfilling a sign; all we need is the sound of the trumpet and look to the eastern sky because our Savior's appearance is nigh.

There are two kinds of people in the USA: those who know Jesus and those who don't. When some run in fear and try to live in their strength and combat the enemy, we, as believers, must give them the message with urgency.

We have been attacked in America and do not know who the enemy is. Still, we see the one who wins the battle, and that is Jesus, so we must reach out and touch that one life that may not know this Jesus because America is in trouble. For our children and grandchildren, we must return to the God of our forefathers and what this country was founded upon, which was a holy God.

America's Children

Tell it to your children, let your children tell it to their children
and their children to the next generation

—Joel 1:3

Many will say we are living in strange times. We are experiencing drought-like conditions never seen before: lakes drying, trees dying, and water scarcity in ways we took for granted. We hear about earthquakes, hurricanes, and many natural disasters, so we may need to look to the Eastern Sky.

There are so many around who show they do not acknowledge a God, only themselves, as we watch children all over becoming a target of sexual predators and men on the internet luring without us as a society to control the usage of a worldwide website.

The needs and attention of America's children have been left by so many divorces, drugs, and parents' sins that drive them into the arms of strangers. They never have a childhood and are moved quickly from the innocence of a child. Homes have become a place to sleep and never eat anymore because of working parents and the activities of the children and the parents.

Parents doing nails, hair, yoga, tanning booths, sports, and workouts have left the children crying for attention. The homes are only houses where we walk through the doors for sleep, baths, maybe eat, watch T.V., and play video games, and children enter a world of exhaustion and confusion not being hugged or having a quiet time with them to talk about their day.

Time has a way of slipping by, and before we know it, God was not taught, church has not attended, and we never hear the words from a pulpit and wonder why the children are so out of control. All this is not an insurance policy that will not go wrong with the child, but it will instill values, and hopefully, they will return to the root of their training.

America and its families have become overwhelmed by all the demands and children not allowed to play in a yard with neighborhood children. We now have computers to supervise because a sexual predator may chat with the child. Do children have any freedom anymore?

Even in our churches, we must know those who might be attracted to our children in youth organizations, Boy Scouts, or any youth gatherings. Parents today must always have radar going and checking on their children.

When the radar is on self as a parent and not the children, children wander and connect to those who will fulfill their needs that parents become so preoccupied with themselves that they do not see the signs. It may be too late to turn around to the children if we do not start in the home at an early age.

If the Church is never attended, Jesus' name is never uttered, values are not taught, then they walk into society needy and confused and searching, and the man or woman will find your children because it will be revealed in the way they dress, where they go, what they say. Destructive behaviors attract bad behavior people.

America is not America the beautiful; it may become America the ugly. When *In God We Trust* is an issue, and our government has not taken a stand to keep God in government, how can we expect this generation of young children to believe in God?

The enemy said he is a roaring lion looking to destroy, and we sit by and let him in our homes and land, missing children and young adults in college, school shootings, rape, drugs; and how can young parents correct this if they are drunk and on drugs inside their walls, where are the children?

When we in America deny self, put children beyond their desires and their flesh, and speak the name of Jesus, maybe Jesus is not at home in them, so how will they ever speak the name of Jesus? America's children are suffering. Wake up America.

Spiritual Warfare In America

The weapons of our warfare are not of the flesh but have
divine power to destroy strongholds.

—2 Corinthians 10:4

Spiritual warfare has become so fierce on earth and among nations. As we walk around, we become aware of people who are angry, impatient, and feeling for their fellow man, who may be a senior citizen, disabled, or just a fellow trying to do his job. We as a society are becoming so non-tolerant, with no respect for life and no feeling for the consequences, so we scream, use our body language, our tongues, cars, guns, or whatever we have to release our displeasure.

We have more money, education, and power but less kindness, love, and patience; You go before me, you can have before me, has become an act lost in this generation. You ask, "What is wrong with the world?" Could it be Satan's tactic to fill your life with his thoughts and your heart with lies and deceit that shows the fruit of your life daily with your fellow man?

Has greed taken over life, and when we mention the name of Jesus, you draw up in a fetal position because you are so afraid to let go of control, and Jesus will ask you to change? Does your guilt enter you, or are you so far into denial that you feel everyone is closing in?

You say, "This is mine, I earned it, and I will not share; I will serve me and myself." The world is full of greed and lack of peace all because your twenty-four-hour day does not acknowledge Jesus in a moment of your day and time.

When will our country and people understand and realize floods in the Big Easy and earthquakes under a sea, fires, and children being murdered by parents and strangers is God shouting to us turn around, America, and fall to your knees and call me by name and I will heal your land and your hearts. Still, in our defiance, we stand with an iron fist in our political offices and homes and deny the one who owns it all.

Why do you think our bodies belong to us when the one who can remove your breathing at any moment waits for us to turn around? Families are parting, neighbors are feuding, children are hurting, guns are used to handle conflict, and drugs are used to numb the mind and heart because coping with reality will not be an option for them.

We must stand tall like Daniel in the lion's den and the three in the furnace, become four with Christ, and not bend; he promises us we will not burn. We have become a lukewarm people, and as parents and grandparents and friends and neighbors, we must realize Satan has become rampant.

We have a society afraid during the day to shop or do the usual routine, and drugs have entered homes and workplaces in places we have no clue about. The internet is an avenue where the intelligent brain steals our personhood, and all control is left with a criminal mind.

There is only one solution to America and our homes, and we must shout to our young to turn back before we slide off the chart of no return. The warning sounds are louder; can you hear them, and can you see them?

What is our priority today? Whenever a generation removes them-selves a little further each day from their creator, we must become aware every hair on your head belongs to him; you are so special to him that He counts them repeatedly.

He knows where that little bird falls; how much more does He love you? He gave His son; will you give your son to somebody just because of love? One day, our control will be lost, and a doctor. may walk into a room and tell us about our health or a loved one. Will our money, drugs, and alcohol provide a way to escape reality?

Cash and your activities will not take away a hospital bed, a nursing home, or a wasted life of regrets, and then you will say, "I wish I had off, I wish I would have…" and there will not be any going back because you cannot have an instant replay to life.

Christ answers every emotion, life experience, and pain in our lives. You take time to go to a movie and take time to go to work; we all take time for those things we want to do, but never open the word and take time to read the letter from Jesus that says He loves you and wants you to have a good life and have a relationship with him.

There are three steps to the peace you are trying to have: admit an honest confession, you and you made the mistakes, not somebody else who made you do it. accept him and believe. We believe in the pilot of a plane that is going to take our life and risk that the aircraft will leave the ground and stay up and then come down safely; why do we trust a pilot all along, the most excellent pilot that needs to be charged is your Lord who knew you in your mother's womb before you were ever born?

Don't wait until your end to trust and believe; let Him be the pilot who flies you to a higher place than you have ever been before, and you will not need the drugs to make you fly and escape a reality that when you awake in the morning, the pain is still there, but with Jesus, the pain will be gone.

What Has Happened To Society?

Righteousness lifts a nation, but sin is a disgrace in any society. Righteousness exalts a nation, and sin is a reproach to any people.

—Proverbs 14:34

What happened, and when did it happen to a society that blushed because of embarrassment? What happened to the respect for life and what happened to *please, thank you, excuse me,* and the rising out of your seat when the respect for the elderly persons needed a place to sit? What happened to the parents' hearts when their children disrespected authorities and parents disciplined them, teachers, and law officials?

We have many broken homes, children crying because of abuse, and the word drug was never used. What happened to us when only Elvis could be seen from the waist up, helping our brother in need and taking the time nobody seems to have today for one another?

What happened to time together to play games? Talk about days of old when children played tag hide and seek, and women joined together as a group to share their hearts, but just because they took time and loved one another and cared?

Have we as a people filled our minds and hearts with noise, drinks, drugs, and things that we have become a lonely society? We have so much more than any society ever: bigger houses, larger automobiles, investments, more and more and bigger and better, and yet we have lost our way searching for a hole to be filled.

We fly to an island and try to have that feel-good vacation with lots of people around us, yet the ache does not go away for the love we all desire. We fill our larger homes with the latest styles, and the closets hang full of fashion that the checkbook and you only know of the cost, yet we are lonely, and the ache does not go away.

We all lay on our pillow of life, then face our own emotions that no one can reach, and then the flood of aches still comes in the empty hole. The hole will never go away or be filled until we as a people get into our deepest selves and let the feeling be natural and not run from the issues of the past, whether a hurt that still lies there from our losses that still linger, or some abuse in a way that hurt us, so we do not ever let the pain be dealt with so we spew our hurts on our fellow man.

A sore is there, and only the name of Jesus will be the salve that, if only applied daily, will heal our sore. If not taken as directed, the infection will come back and back again until we go to the root problem and let JESUS pour his healing oil into the infected sore.

You may then lay your head down at night and will not need to run, shop until you drop, and go to all the quick fixes you have run to and peace like a river will flood your soul, so the need will not be a need anymore all because you chose to go to the source that supplies all your needs.

We become so exhausted as a society trying to find the answer to life and having that feel-good feeling when in the end only leaves us still searching. We never discovered nor did anyone ever tell you the answer is found in Christ and Christ alone.

Where Are The Revivals For America?

Will you revive us again, that your people may rejoice in you?

—Psalm 85:6

With men today so vile, disobedient, unthankful, and unholy, why doesn't the church have more revivals? As a child, I remember revivals in our little country church where there were no funds, only love offerings, no great structure, nobody dressed in the finest attire, but loved the Lord and loved him so much they invited people to come and would walk the isles to speak to those they knew were lost.

I heard many testimonies of how they loved Jesus, and tears flowed, and shouting erupted, and I never looked at a clock. Their concern was nobody going to Hell and loving Jesus. I remember my mother frying chicken and inviting the preachers home to dinner (lunch now). And we had nothing, but Mom would cook a feast.

We as a society have become so social that we have forgotten it is all about prayer, love, concern, hope, empathy, and servanthood. We are so busy in this materialistic world with children, activities, houses, jobs, and things that serve ourselves that we have hardened our hearts so much, and our ears have become deaf to the spirit calling that revival doesn't last long even when they are conducted.

We enter back into the world, and this overpowers our desire for Jesus. When revival comes and our behavior and focus change, we begin to know Jesus is the real focus and true revival has come, then change begins.

When we as a church see children, teenagers, and our friends and family going to hell, then become concerned enough to love, care, and have empathy instead of judgment and stop walking on by. We have revival one at a time, caring, loving, and forgiving, so my prayer today is to let revival begin in me, and maybe I'll let someone see Jesus in me, and they will want what I have.

Part Six

God's Technology

Dear reader,

Idols. What is the first image that pops into your head? The Golden Calf, a car, money—what about your device clutched in the palm of your hand? Technology is the golden calf of our time. We type in or speak a string of words, wanting answers to our questions, and in an instant, it gives us everything we could imagine and more, so why do we need God?

The Word of God warns us not to run faster than we have strength, to look to God and live, to love God and to love thy neighbor as thyself, and to quiet our minds and Be Still. Does technology help us do this, or does it distract us from it?

Humanity's weakness makes us zombie-like forces bowing our heads towards the monitors, phones, tablets, and screens—our God. Gaming, shopping, chatting, pornography, and disengaging from reality allow our brains to get dopamine hits with each mouse click and strike of the keyboard, so why wouldn't we use it?

"People will be lovers of themselves… lovers of pleasure rather than lovers of God," 1 Timothy 3: 1-5. We are here with technology.

In this section, you will see how my heart cried out to warn others, but no one seemed to hear it. It's like I'm walking in a dreamish nightmare where the people I love are distracted and connected to the God in their hands. They were all connected to a device instead of each other. It is not a dream when I wake up and go outside; this nightmare is absolute.

Please put down the device no matter what, get on your knees, and bow your head to the true and everlasting God.

Electronic Madness

Therefore, having these promises, beloved, let us cleanse ourselves from all filthiness of the flesh and spirit, perfecting holiness in the fear of God.

—1Corinthians 7:1

iPods, PlayStation, and all gadgets with different names leave me like my forefathers. Not even knowing if an airplane could fly and how the TV came through the air to reveal a picture? I am shopping today for grandchildren and reading the Christmas list, and it leaves me confused because I do not know what they are asking for.

Satan knew to use the computer, yet the Lord also used it to preach to all. The world that proves you can take something intended for good and abuse what it was designed for.

When we give the children all the gadgets that for hours occupy their minds and do not exercise their bodies, we pay the price of a generation of children to be fed messages in their little minds of violence, aggression, sex, and no respect for life. We have watched young adults and children camping out for PlayStation 3, and the desire is so great that they are willing to stand in the cold, steal, or whatever it takes to have this game.

Are these games used for babysitting so parents will not be bothered, or is Satan luring our Children into an unknown world? What messages are being sent that would make them Desire to sit for two days to acquire this little instrument? Do we give them a gift that will carry the children?

Through the hard times and last forever and will minister to their souls, or do we give them the Electronic instrument to keep their minds so focused that no thought will be had about their Creator?

Our children and grandchildren are lost in a world where we sit idly by and watch these Electronics for hours and never learn how to have relationships to skip rope, play tag, and use The imagination of their minds, where an electronic machine has replaced.

The reason is the guide To what you think, and our children are craving all these gadgets, but when life's hurts appear, Will their machine fix the pain?

As young parents teach them values and monitor what goes into their little minds, they wonder why aggression and acts of drugs and alcohol appear In their teenagers. We are now reaping the consequences of our youth and desires for electronics. The minds and hearts have become numb to right and wrong, so who is to blame?

Where is Jesus being taught and the values of life in all the electronics, so why are we surprised at the increase of problems of our youth? When young parents get off the throne and wake up to their children's desires for things that occupy their minds and not their hearts, we will turn this America around.

God was taken out of society, so there will be pain, conflicts, and confusion, and it keeps on with a mouse and a game until we do not need to turn around or feel we are doing anything wrong, so the cycle goes on. Wake up, America and parents, unplug the electronic madness, and let silence be had so your children will know the value of life. Be still for a while. You might find the peace you desire.

God Has An E-Mail Address

WWW.JESUS.COM

You, therefore, my son, be strong in the grace in Christ Jesus
and the things that you have heard from me among many
witnesses, and commit these to faithful men who will be able
to teach others also.

—2 Timothy 2:1

We all have an e-mail address today, and we want our message to reach the other person like a bolt of lightning, and we want it to be faster and faster and have our message be received in a speedy world.

We send other people e-mail messages and forward them so everyone knows the news simultaneously. Just like an e-mail address, Jesus wants us to use his e-mail and send a message. He wants it to come fast by his word and inform us today there needs to be a meeting and wants us all to attend.

When we feel that his little letter is in our spirit, we will not click and go in and open the message. We delete the icon and an essential message that could change the day we live.

Most of us carry around viruses like a computer and say to ourselves we can fix this problem, so we go around in life, hitting the shutdown button, hitting escape, and shutting off the power that wants to be our power and never open our email to our souls and get the message from the greatest of all help desk for our life.

The busy world of our computers has replaced quietness and time with our lord, who also wants to be a source of information that only he can ever give.

Satan's Technology

Do you not know that you are the temple of God, and the
spirit of God dwells in you?

—1 Corinthians 3:18

In this world of the 20th and 21st centuries, we all have computers;
we can click once, and it takes us to games. Click again, find out what
our securities are worth, and we may even go to a chat room and chat
for a while; we are all alike. We race to every website within ourselves,
occupying our minds with all the garbage we can, so like the computer,
we build our minds so we need more rams or bites to go faster, do more,
and be better.

Our lives take us to escapes that make us live in the noise of the
world where God cannot be heard. We want to know about the Dow
and whether interest rates go up, so we browse the internet and find all
the answers to all our questions, all along trying to make a machine reach
our security for life in an insecure world.

We all have bigger houses than our forefathers, fine cars, and all the
glitter and toys. We think this gives us security, but as a generation, we
have less than our parents and grandparents because they stopped on
Sunday for a God. They visited the sick family and helped their fellow
man fill the void in their lives.

We don't find anybody at home anymore; they may be napping from
a sixty-hour week when only forty were to be working.

As hundreds of automobiles pass us by, we toot our horns, now to say hello, but in rage because we are in a hurry to the deadlines in our lives that we think are a priority. Like pressure pots without an air valve, we run in the rush of life, filling our lives with the world's busyness.

Satan knows if he could keep us busy and take over the strongholds of our minds, we as a society would leave our God, and he would own our time and our day, and then when we hit the pain of life, where the escapes of this world cannot be solved, where we thought all the security was, it is only then if we stop, we can maybe hear a small voice say, stop, look to me, I'm your security, not man, not 401k, not the Dow, not those malls you run to and escape, believe me and my word, I am your friend in these times of trouble.

I will be your peace in this rat race of life, so shut off your search engine, turn off the noise, and try me says Jesus, I will give you all that information you are searching so desperately to find.

So Much And So Little

Whose mouths must be stopped, who subvert the whole households, teaching things which they ought not, for the sake of dishonest gain.

—Titus 1:11

As I read your word, Lord, I became aware our society is so noisy and fast we cannot be still long enough and quiet in a world of high technology. We can numb our minds by surfing and going places our families are unaware of. This is an escape that fills us with Satan's tactics to lure us away from anything Godly.

Loving God with all our hearts and minds and thinking upon things lovely is only if anything is left over from a busy and hurried mind. Sometimes we wonder what thinking things delightful means when news of shootings, robbing, raping, missing children, and abuse is on the rise.

Our world has become like the days of old when God got fed up and set the floods and famines to the people in the Old Testament, and now we see hurricanes and earthquakes under a sea beyond our imagination. And could God be fed up with sin? Even Christians are living their life without the total dependency on the Lord.

They seem to have all that money can buy and fill their days with thoughts of retirement or the get-rich-quick idea, and all along, they leave their God who created and gave it all to them.

The God they serve will not mend a broken heart, cure a deadly disease, or give peace like a river. We have more people and more money, more glamor, and more noise, and yet people who need more drugs, alcohol, or an addiction of some sort that tries to give the high so the feeling will not be felt. This society has filled its days with malls, exercising, and everything that lures us to satisfy a craving and desire that the world will never give.

Where is the lighthouse in us to draw people to learn more about Jesus? There may be a lonely heart and disturbed mind around us just waiting for a gentle touch or voice to affirm Christ, and we love them. We communicate in our lives that God is love and loves us all. He wants us to have peace, joy, and an abundant life no matter what we have done.

May a caring heart, a phone call, a card, or a hug just be a need they have, and they are afraid to express the neediness of their heart for fear no one understands them. When they see what Christ means to us and how he carries us through the valleys, our light is not hidden under the bushel, but we is the salt that heals a broken heart.

When our suffering makes us relate to our fellow man and gives us compassion for a person in their valley, then we can express our love. Then they realized we went traveling in other directions. This road leads to a real God who gave us His all, His Son, and shows them their Gods don't last, but our God is accurate and true.

The Internet Of God

What profit is the image, that it makes should carve it, the molded image, a teacher of lies, that the maker of its mold should trust in it, to make a mute idols?

—Habakkuk 2:18

We all go online to pull up a search engine that searches for the questions in our minds. We search and click until we arrive at the place that gives us the answers to those things we are searching for. We learn things we never knew before; it is so full of information.

We can travel across the oceans and nations and have become an intelligent technology society, but are we? We have become a society that will not use their internet search engines to search and seek a God who made them and gave them their very life. Do our search engines on our computers help us when death or loss arrives?

We cannot get past our pain, and then our hurting hearts linger like a burn from a flame. Do we go to a chat room and chat for a while because we are so lonely and our crying heart needs a friend who can share, and nobody will know our real needs?

Yes, we are an intelligent society, going to the moon, making computers that have helped us to escape the problems that lie so deep within us all, occupying places we want to go, and so for a little while, we run that little message from our email which Christ, wants to give.

We are so intelligent that when we get a message from someone who can answer all our questions, we escape it. When disappointments, pain, and heartaches come, if we would only click on the name of Jesus and receive his message, then He would 186 reveal all the information we are looking for, and no viruses will ever shut Him down and make Him crash.

This is what our search engine is looking for, and we do not even know it, so let your mind be filled with the answer which lies with JESUS and stop surfing the net where you will never find what you are looking for, and don't let the busy world lure you into a life of no return.

Get out of the chat rooms and chat with one who will fill a friendship and all the emotions you are trying to fill. Try Him. He does not fail you like a man and everything you have been attempting to fill the hole that lies so deep within your soul.

The Silence Of Satan

For this is the will of God, that by doing good you may put to silence the ignorance of foolish men.

—1 Peter 2:15

How can something so tiny destroy a life? Satan knew when he conquered the mind, so goes the world. The computer age is a weapon against the family of our nation and the world. Man has become so intelligent that we have outsmarted ourselves.

Every year, a new chip is created, one that searches the worlds of knowledge and, in a click, goes faster than the blink of an eye. It goes to unknown worlds for most of us and to places man has never gone before.

Children are caught watching porn, and us telling them never to speak to strangers. Yet, parents allow the busy world of computers and individuals to receive a visit from our children and grandchildren that brings the sexual imagination of the mind that destroys lives forever. Transferring millions of dollars, watching pornography, gambling from addiction with monies beyond the limit, and because of the creation of the chip now creates many habits for society.

People search the web and do not search for Christ to fill their void and try to find a chat room that allows their minds to escape the pressures of this life we live. Young children not monitored by parents and living in blended families have proven that we are living in an unknown world because of the internet.

All people and all kinds can acquire the internet without those they know to be aware of the condition of their heart. Be sure your sins will find you out, and if that mind has addictions, it can be had on the internet. Satan knows the weakest link between the sinful nature of man. So, man allows the click of a mouse to go to a site not centered around Christ.

Satan makes the mind sink into desires. Some do not have the passion, strength, and wisdom to hit the escape button and shut it down, so the addiction cost them their lives and many more lives around them. Little girls and little goys are lured by so-called chat rooms and by men with wrong intentions in their hearts and yielded by temptation.

You may be a Christian or non-Christian, but man is always tempted because we are flesh and sin that, when ingested, goes to the crevices of our being, and no matter the tears, there will never be a return to the life we have known.

Man is deceived by a spirit that is a war against the principalities and spirits not seen by man, and all along, the chip is chipping away that was only designed for knowledge, but because of sin, it is used as a weapon of mass destruction.

We have heard these words from our president many times recently, but the descent is in our homes with the internet. We can take a mouse and click on it, and transfer funds across the oceans, outsource jobs, speak to strangers in foreign lands and think our children are doing homework etc. Those clicks of the mouse are done with doors closed and chatting to some strange individual who does not have their best interest in mind. The illusion of a sick mind and yet, all along, one of intelligence who can go to the websites of us do not even have a clue luring our children.

Children are so naive and innocent, and when strangers promise them things that their parents will not permit, they fall to that temptation—a desire inside to connect to the site on the internet and tell a stranger the problems of their heart. Those who receive the message are ready to receive their news, say the words, and take our children on a journey of no return.

Parents need to wake up, get rid of themselves, and save their children before we lose this generation. Let them connect to the source that will keep your family and create in your children sound values, and live a life before them so that by your example, they will want to chat with only you and will not be so needy in their room of secrets chatting with strangers.

Children need safe people in their lives, who we hope are parents and grandparents who will instill in children a healthy mind so they will know values and have respect for God's chat room, which is the bible and church, and learn what true love is and not out there in cyberspace. May we as adults open our eyes, reach the level of alarm, unplug the chat rooms from our children and grandchildren, and block Satan's lure for the children.

Until parents take control of the mouse, children will not have access to the interests of all the tactics of Satan to destroy our homes. We must put on the alarm just like in our homes so that when you, as parents, see the signs and the alarm goes off, hear the sound and check it out because the life you may save may be your child.

Part Seven

Leaning On God's Word

Dear Reader,

The Word. Scriptures. The Good Book. All these titles bring us back to one place—where God spoke to Man and shared information, directions, warnings, encouragement, poetry, sternness, and love. We have a very tangible place where God's Word is there for us to consume and integrate into our lives.

Reading the scripture is foundational to learning how God loves His children—all of us. The Book is there for all to grasp, open, and allow our minds to be influenced by His answers to our prayers, longings, pain, and questions. The Word of God is God's way of talking directly to you.

The Word changes hearts, minds, and lives when we follow and obey the counsel given. We are fundamentally changed because when the deity speaks to you, it is like a mighty rushing wind penetrating your soul. The imprint of God has stirred your soul, and you have a secret. The secret is that you know right from wrong.

You know the better choice, and Satan and his minions will do all they can to confuse you—turn you away from the word and try to numb you or root it out of your breast with all manner of poor decisions, guilt, and shame. But never-the-less, the Lord has stirred your soul, and the truth is imprinted there, and it will remain there. My encouragement is not to fight it—embrace it!

In this section, you will read the impact scripture has on my soul—where my soul turns to find hope and love from the pain and heartache of the world. My prayer is that you will read these examples and find your soul remembering to turn to The Word and discover His light again in your life.

A Day Of The Signs

But of that day and how no one knows, not even the angels of heaven, but my father only. But as the days of Noah were so also will the coming of the son of man be.

—Matthew 24:36-37

When we see the signs of your coming lord, we feel the presence of your spirit and know you are omnipresent and all-knowing, so you give us peace and hope. As I witness my friend's baptism (September 20, 2005), I am moved by Your drawing of the Holy Spirit

Others ride along on a raft of life with the ocean and all the rafts, never realizing how the waves draw. The ride seems safe, but it draws us further from shore. As we see the shore going off in the distance, the shock fills our bodies when we have drifted so far and not realizing we were very comfortable and peaceful, having fun and enjoying the ride and not alert to our surroundings and how far from shore we have drifted.

We then, in panic, cry out, lord help, and he throws out the lifeline and the life preserver to us. And we reach hard, crying, and we must move toward it and grab hold of him and not go the opposite direction, and the Lord then pulls us in, and we feel the tremendous relief of safety and peacefulness that we have been rescued from danger.

As we watch nature and its power of the sun rising at a specific time, the tide knowing its destiny, the birds know when to feed, and I see one lonely little pigeon laying before me with a hurt foot, and as I throw the crumbs, the pigeon seems grateful. I compare myself to the Lord, throwing him my crumbs and wanting him to have the whole slice, but in my flesh, I drift like the raft of life and give him just the crumbs.

Nature reminds me of your Power, Lord, your creation, and the control of every grain of sand and ocean waves. If you have that control over the ocean, how much more do you control me and my environment and this earth? Are you pulling the curtain down and saying this day is over, and have I given the Lord the slice or the crumbs?

Lord, help me when things are out of control. May I turn to the one who controls all this ocean and nature and trust you. Put a guard over my mouth, and let you be the captain of my ship and not tell you where to go or how to drive the boat. I just need you to be on board and let me navigate the water of life, and only then will I experience the tranquility of peace like a river you want to give me.

I praise you for giving me this day.

A God Of Miracles

God also bearing witness both with signs and wonders, with
various miracles, and the gift of the holy spirit according to
his own will.

—Hebrews 2:4

Again, I stand in awe, Lord, at your provision. You're constantly being on time. My son experienced a mighty God, and thank you for the buyer in a prolonged market, in a new subdivision where many new houses were.

Still, they chose to buy this house and then to provide the money that we did not have to get involved in, provide a rental person understanding enough to let them move their furniture in, and then the driver's license he begged you to find and how many times do you have to reveal an awesome God and answered prayers.

Lord, I also marvel at your goodness and never want to forget what a God we serve while times may be suitable.

I remember reading in your Word how you performed many miracles, and then the people would forget, so Lord, help me never to forget a God who helps in times of trouble.

You are my rock, and I stand on your promises, so Lord, help me today to remember when I cried out when I thought I could not go on another mile and I said have mercy on me; you heard my cry, and thank you does not seem to be enough and I praise your holy name, Amen.

Attending God's University

The name of the Lord is a strong tower, the righteous run to it and are safe, the rich man's wealth is a strong city, and like a high wall in his own esteem.

—Proverbs 18:10

Do we cry sometimes and say, "Lord, I do not want to take my hands off that because I am afraid, and this is my security? This is all about me, Lord; please don't make me give you that." My friends and family do not understand. I say, "Lord, what will I do with my life now if I give you that?"

As we become older and until we are taken off the *merry-go-round* of life, it gets faster and faster; then He put me in His university to teach me about himself, and the flood of tears came gushing from all the years of pain. I then realized He wanted to talk with me in my aloneness with Him, no phone calls, no TV, and just the quietness of my home.

I was just where He wanted me to be. He used tools like friends who encouraged me to read the book Battlefield of the Mind, so I did. I began to go into God's word and read and read with passion. I knew Jesus in my heart, but there was a battle about how I think and react to certain situations. I stayed His Word for days, reading and praying, because Satan knew my mind, and he knew if he could keep that for himself, I would never live in victory.

I filled my mind with as many of his promises as I could. I went very slowly to have His Word reveal what God wanted to say, and then I just said boldly, "Okay, God, I cannot do this in my flesh; I need you to reveal what is happening." I then turned to Romans 8:32, "If I have given my son to die for you, how much more will I do for you? And a gush went all over me, and a revelation came to my spirit that I had never known or felt before."

That is the secret: Christ owns my mind also. He wants me not to be defeated, and with His power in my mind and all over my body, if I do not get that message engraved in my mind, then I say to Him *His death was all in vain.*

There was a release in me beyond my explanation, and after all the tears, praying, and asking, I never went outside my home until HE revealed this to me, just me and Him in the garden.

He revealed to me that my mind was filled with emotions, scared from the past, full of self-taught ideas, and some from things that happened to me along life's journey, whether it was school, neighbors, church, friends, or parents.

We are all programmed like a computer, and a computer shuts down all because of too much information, and so goes our minds. We must watch what goes on and protect our minds. Christ speaks in His Word, renews the mind-breaking strongholds, and breaks the bondage that holds us, and we never realize as children and adults, we are programmed to think thoughts that were taught by the world and not Christ's thoughts.

When we try to change our flesh, we must realize this cannot be done without Christ and His Word and reprogramming. If we have a willing heart and let Christ enter those crevices that linger from our childhood and taught behaviors, only then will we have the sound mind and abundant life HE wants for each one of us.

We can only have a renewed mind once we go to Him. In this age, being still and quiet is a rare moment in this busy and noisy world, and how can we hear Him if we cannot be still and quiet?

When we repent, be genuine and honest with Him; we seek, knock, and ask, and the door will be opened. He will come in if we have a willing heart and take the risk of facing the pain that we act out in our behaviors to try to escape facing it and the one who made you.

Only we can have the victory and freedom we desire, and the truth will set you free to turn to Jesus and let Him change your mind and mindset. Then, you will begin to live a life with purpose and meaning.

Deep Waters

When you pass through waters I will be with you and through the rivers, they shall not overflow you when you walk through the fire, you shall not be burned.

—Isaiah 43:2

As we read the scripture, I will be with you when you walk through the waters. I am reminded of a mother with hospice in my home and watching a loving saint face death so bravely, and I remember her asking, "How long does it take to wither away?" I knew she had assurance with her Lord, but how many of us who walk when that time arrives will smile, have peace, and not go into a depressed state?

When we know him personally as our friend, we will all face the bad news with assurance of where we are and where we are going. There are more and more signs of His return, and we must rest assured and work toward the day we will be raptured, or He will take us home through some life experience.

We have more technology, better doctors, and health care, yet cancer and the common cold cannot be cured. Cancer has become increasingly common, and yet man, in all his studies, cannot find the cure. Could this be because the Lord does not want us to control all things like man struggles to do today?

Man has more knowledge, has more machines, and has more finances than any generation before, and yet we are a sick society. We work long hours to accumulate wealth, take pills, drink, take drugs, and have all the gadgets that keep being invented, and yet we run to the doctor for help.

The media just announced a record number of people taking sleeping pills and becoming where they cannot sleep. Could this society be not sleeping because of a lost generation that has never wanted to know a Christ who can help the mind be at peace with their environment?

Maybe we will let go of the desires of our heart for things, places, and all the lures that never fulfill that place in our soul that was only created for a Lord to enter. It will never be filled with all of the above, so when you take Jesus three times a day, you will not need to call a doctor to sleep, and you will not take a pill and call him in the morning; He is on call twenty-four seven so let Him be your doctor for a while and see one by one all the issues of your life change. He wants to love you; why do you not wish for Him? Nothing else is working.

*(Special Note: This is my life verse through many valleys with the death of loved ones.)

Do We Take Up Our Cross Daily?

But God forbid that I should boast except in the cross of our
Lord Jesus Christ, by whom, the world has been crucified to
me and I to this world.

—Galatians 6:14

Taking up our cross daily is a new beginning for each of us; we can forget yesterday and live for Christ just today. We must come to a place where we know a Christ-like, our very best friend, and only then will we have the peace we desperately seek.

We cannot express our thoughts about our destiny and struggles with our lives because we do not want anyone to know the real us that lies so profoundly inside, yet our behavior exposes the condition of our hearts. We have fears and insecurities and a lack of peace, yet we do not want to share the real us all because we fear rejection. We want to make sure to be accepted, but we don't think about being accepted by a Christ who gives his all.

The last time we may have trusted someone, they betrayed us, so we tell our minds we will not go there again. We keep all inside, spew out our anger or pent-up emotions, and live a life of defeat.

Christ hopes while in the state of mind, a person will come along their way to tell them about Him because He was born and died to free us all from the garbage we hold on to, and when we understand and accept Him, only then will we have this peace that passeth all understanding that we desire so desperately.

Every Valley Makes Me Love You More

For we know that the whole creation groans and labors with birth pangs together until now.

—Romans 8:22

We all want a life of ease with no pain, no struggles, and no mountains to climb, but life does not allow this place to last long. Each one must face the unknown, and when a turn of events throws us to face death's door of ourselves or a loved one, we then experience a true living God.

In those valleys looking up to a mountain too high to climb, we find ourselves so much dependent on God, Him holding us up out of those deep waters and not letting the fire set us ablaze, for He is our God.

We face circumstances beyond our control, and we all face fears and stresses of this life with illness, divorces, grandchildren, job losses, and losses of many kinds. When we are in those valleys and go to the rock and His Word, we read all about those promises like, I will never leave you nor forsake you.

Our relationship becomes so real, He wants our heart to feel His love, and the presence of His Spirit. In every valley, we learn to love Him more and more, and we learn to trust Him. He gives us peace amid the trial, and His sweet spirit rests in our soul beyond the words man expresses.

When amid a storm, we can praise Him, and then the peace that passeth all understanding is given and carries us all the way. It is in those times of deep waters we love you more. When our circumstances touch lives, we realize there is a plan and purpose for all things so someone else will see Jesus in us, which is the purpose of all things.

When in deep waters, we trust more, love more, wait more, seek more, so Lord, in your time, not ours, Lord, we depend on you and because we know a mountain is not a mountain to you, so today we praise you for the valley because you have proven yourself to us over and over again.

You have a love beyond understanding, so yes, Lord, in the valley, we love you more today, yesterday, and tomorrow; we can hear a voice saying, "Do not fear, Trust Me, Wait on the Lord."

I am doing a new thing, so keep my flesh at bay and keep self from rising its head, and may I dwell with you in times like these. People need the Lord so they may see Jesus in me.

Good Stuff Buried Deep

Again, the kingdom of heaven is like a merchant seeking beautiful pearls; who when he had found one pearl a great price, went and sold all that he had and bought it.

–Matthew 13:45

I have heard it said, "Why does God bury all the good stuff of value? We have to dig and labor to find it, like oil, water, gold, diamonds, coal, etc., where it is ours for the taking."

We must also search for all the good stuff God has created for us. We cannot lay back and say, "I have accepted you, so Lord, bring it to me." We believe we work and earn; God will just give us what we ask, but He also makes us go through the storms and fires to see if we mean what we say.

Today, Help us learn in valleys, storms, and the fire to hear your promise; I will be with you because you never said I would take all this from you.

Just like the search for precious metals and jewels, our jewel is the person of Jesus. We must dig in the Word, pray with our being, and seek and ask for wisdom to find life's meaning. We must listen with spiritual ears and see with His eyes. We must heed the warnings that keep us on the path toward Him and not down the road of destruction and never be able to turn around.

A diamond is dirty and in many odd forms and must be cleaned, hammered, and beaten to bring a light of beauty to our lives. We must allow Jesus to cleanse and mold us into the jewel He has hidden deep inside our dirty lives.

Only He can make clean the sparkling jewel He knows he has created. He has a purpose, and each of us is unique, just like jewels, no one alike. It takes some longer to be found, to be cleaned and hammered. We must be willing to be hammered, and only then will Jesus make us a creation of beauty.

Our light will shine, and others may see Jesus in us. It is not metals of monetary value Jesus is after; it is to see how hard we want to dig and how far we want Him to hammer and mold us to make us that light and jewel of beauty.

We may remain dirty and hidden, but Jesus knows where you are in all that dirt. We are His creation and glory, but we must realize our worth and believe we have beauty beyond all the earth.

You must let Jesus find you and know your worth; He died, so you do not need to live in the dirt. We must not lay there and live a wasted life when we were created, and nobody can see the beauty like Jesus and know your worth like Jesus.

Man cannot ever see your price like Jesus. We are today into extreme makeovers because we think beauty is on the outside; when Jesus sees your beauty inside, like the gems in the dirt, let Jesus dig you out, shine you, and mold you because you will never sparkle in this sinful world.

We will continually struggle and feel pain because we never let the one find us and validate our beauty and worth. Man does not know your soul, heart, head, or secret thoughts. They are buried just like all the metals and gems, and only Jesus knows where you are, just like the jewels.

When all your pain, conflicts, and bondage cannot be solved, turn to the one who knows your way down deep. Let Jesus uncover the dirt, hold you, and mold you; only then will your self-worth be found.

The stuff of this world will not matter anymore because you will have the peace and love you are looking for, so why lay there in the dirt today when Jesus wants you to rise to the top in this life and be a beautiful diamond he created. Only Jesus can give you that gift.

My God Is An Awesome God

So now our God, the great and mighty and awesome God
who keeps his covenant and love.

—Nehemiah 9:32

My God is incredible. He gave us the ocean, the sunrise, birds, and all creatures to enjoy. The peace that roars inside me like ocean waves is beyond my words. The beauty of a light over the calmness of the sea and the rays of a reflection upon the water's edge reveals the rays that peek its head inch by inch, and then the flow of a sun appears.

I am amazed at the on-time Lord and His power to make the sunrise at the precise moment. He also pulls me like the tide from the trials of every day, and yet there is peace as we feel by the seaside.

When the storms make the pounding of the waves and an angry sea, so do storms in our life come, and yet there is One who controls the highs and lows of our life just like the ocean tides.

As we see the pelicans fly in order and glide and know when to dive to feed upon fish, the Lord also knows when to attack me and provide me His Word and more of HIM. With every new day, HIS light becomes more evident, that in me, He is revealing HIMSELF and who holds the future.

If the sand, the foul, and the waves are in his control, how much more does HE control me? I am looking now at the eastern sky, and one day, it will not be this quiet; it will be with a bursting forth, and everyone will look up, and the waves will stop their roar, and the birds will cease their flights, and we will see a SAVIOR THAT COMES FOR US.

It is a love more significant than this ocean and knows me more than the grains of this sand. GLORY TO GOD IN THE HIGHEST, GREAT THINGS HE HAS DONE. AMEN

My Rock

The Lord Lives! Blessed be my rock! Let God be exhausted, the rock of my salvation.

—2 Samuel 22:47

My rock, my refuge, my present help in times of trouble. That is what you are to me, Lord, today as I watch a child removed from me by distance, and distances of emotion and spirit also flood my soul where no one can reach but you, Lord.

My children were my life, and I was always giving, loving, serving, and now just me and my spouse. Grandchildren removed in the confines of my home by the sins that a parent chose to trod and not your way but the way of the tempter that destroyed everything in its path and now know what the scripture means, like a roaring lion going around devouring everything and destroying good, but Lord you told us to stomp on our enemies head, and I can do all things through you Lord who strengthens me.

All of my days, the evil one has tried to destroy me through my parents, through abortions, rock music, lies, deceit, cover-ups, robbing me of peace, affairs, re-marriage, grandchildren, deaths, and terrible deaths, watching those die and giving over an ounce of my strength until I see them wither away.

Oh, the memories of hurt and pain flood me again and as they resurface. A child or, let's say, children struggling against behaviors of this world and how they yield, and then, Lord, you intervene when I think it's all over, and you again prove your love and provision for my heart and soul.

When I've given my all to investments in this life and who I helped and loved and is misunderstandings and wrong words told in a false verbal tongue, I now know what a spark of a language which sets life all ablaze means, so Lord, there is no misunderstanding in you Lord.

You understand every word and every word I don't say, yet you love me just as I am. When sin enters, it separates and destroys; that is what I am experiencing. I opened your word today, and you roared; nothing is impossible for God. I surrender my all; all is gone, and I have been stripped of some people's love.

I cannot explain; I cannot make it suitable for the hearts have grown cold and hard, so Lord Satan is the father of all lies, and you are more significant than all the world, so I am today releasing my thoughts, reactions, and behaviors to the Lord who is the great physician.

You will heal my hurts, not man. You will never fail me like man, you will comfort me, you will bless me, for man is flesh and you are spirit, so I yield to you, Lord, to god be the glory for what you have done, what you will do and I praise you, Lord.

Signs Of The End

And he said, Look, I am making known to you, what shall happen in the latter time of the indignation, for at the appointed time the end shall be.

—Daniel 8:19

Every day, we hear of global warming, fires in California, mudslides, floods in the Midwest, and drought in the East. In the secret places of our minds, we all know something is changing in America. We hear of police officers gunned down and no respect for life for authority.

Our children are not safe inside the homes or out in the yards without adult supervision when our generation was free to roam freely. Our homes were our refuge, and playing was a release, and now children are taught in schools at a very early age to guard against drugs, alcohol, sex, etc., to survive in this world. Our schools have become war zones, and our homes are houses of many strangers.

So many have lived with boyfriends and children whose fathers are missing from their homes, leaving a generation of children confused, depressed, and angry. Our young people are on drugs, robbing innocent people to feed their habits, and all our officials are overwhelmed by the volume and set free many among us in our society.

The internet with gambling, pornography, and chat rooms with children has become a sign of the days we live, and we say to ourselves in denial, oh, it has always been this way. Many in America are hungry and cold, with no insurance, no jobs, and homeless, yet America is the land of the free.

Our jobs are sent overseas, leaving many people in line at the unemployment offices and without funds for a family. Are we free, or have we become like Sodom and Gomorrah when we left our God in the schools, government, and homes?

We as a society see the result of this choice. We have no conviction of adultery, sex before marriage, abortions, drinking, drugs, children used for sex, and so on.

Abortions have eliminated a generation of children, and God has been removed from the hearts and this generation will be the leaders of our country sooner than we think.

God, church, or family do not teach them to say I am sorry, remorse for right and wrong, Thank you, and respect for authority, including parents. Can God ever be restored to these children before it is too late?

The earth is becoming hotter because of so many vehicles that help the melting away of the ice in Alaska, Iceland, and the North Pole inhibited animals, and fishing was a source of income for the land. The ice has broken, and danger lurks around all the hunters because of melting; the ocean is rising due to the melting, which will affect the shorelines. Our ancestors never experienced this, so why deny that the Lord is coming soon?

There is an urgency to this message, and there is one who can solve all the chaos and give peace amid the madness, and his name is Jesus. He is the anchor and the lighthouse that will lead us to shore when the ship is sinking. He wants all to be saved and to believe in Him, not this world that is quickly fading away.

God must return to the hearts of His people, and only then will freedom ring in America and its people be free. The end times are raising its ugly head, and we as a church and people must reach out and throw out the lifeline to the lost and hurting souls. I pray that whoever is reading this now will take hold of the rope, let Jesus save you, and pull you to himself before it is too late.

The Bride, The Church

I will rejoice greatly in the Lord; my soul shall be joyful in my God, for he has clothed me with the garment of salvation. He has covered me with the robe of righteousness. As a bridegroom decks himself with ornaments and or a bride adorns herself with her jewels.

—Isaiah 61:10

When the Lord mentions the bride, the people form a church, not a building. There was not any brick & mortar, only a people who, in their humanness, followed not their feelings but a belief that a God could part the Red Sea, and He did.

There is a God who could see through a soul and guide Joseph through valleys, pain, and trials, and yet in the end, there was a plan for life, and Joseph never let go of God. God said in His return, He would come and get His bride.

Is the bride of our churches real, or are they full of rituals, ceremonies, and busyness that they fail to see one beside us on the pew hurting? The one that is unlike us is feeling rejected, and are we judging the external appearance, just like our daily walk with the lord, and failing to get to know our brother enough to understand his needs?

When we fail to see our church grow, it may be that the Lord has increased weary of trying to enter the hearts of His people and trying to see who has a broken and contrite heart, compassionate heart, and repentant heart. Are we busy trying to control each other or judge our brother who failed on the day to see that I have a problem?

Maybe some of us were raised in a home where we had no control, and perhaps abuse of some kind was displayed, and we became a Christian, and yet a lot of our learned behavior from our little girl or little boy is displayed in a committee, an office or maybe just a church member.

Instead of passing me by and seeing the external, stop a minute to get to know me. Don't judge me by the way I dress, drive, or what I show externally a wealth of knowledge. I may be crying inside, wanting you to love, accept, approve, and care about me because I might be lonely. I might be sick, or I might be fearful, and I might be locked up inside, and you just might have the key to unlock me.

We must watch our words and try to ask ourselves before speaking: would this embarrass me or make me feel bad or make you feel more insecure in your self-righteousness projection, making me think I cannot measure up to your standards?

Greet me with love, a hug, and a kind word, and elevate me about something good that I have done or you have seen. I may not be as secure as you; I may not be as pretty as you. I may not know the bible like you, I may not pray like you, and I may not be able to express my feelings like you.

I may have been taught not to share my thoughts and feel like you. I may have been told not to tell, or I may not have had the stable upbringing as you, but I have a heart changed by the Lord just like you.

The Mountain Is Level Ground For God

Your righteousness is like the great mountains; your judgments are a great deep; O Lord, you preserve man and beast.

—Psalm 36:6

When we look at circumstances all around us, it seems like a mountain from all sides, and we do not see a way around, over, or under; we become overwhelmed. We must look back at that moment where we have been and who carried us through until now.

A mountain is not a mountain to God; it is level ground, so we must get to know this God who knows every breath we take and every hair on our head, then our hearts will lighten. It will lift us to heights like the deer that leaps, so our heart leaps in hope, joy, and peace, knowing a mountain is not a mountain to you, Lord.

You are not surprised by the heartaches and circumstances of our lives. It is like a hot iron hammering us into the desired individual we had planned from the beginning of our lives. May we all allow you to beat us into who you want us to be, and maybe those we meet will also want to know this God we serve.

When we know that you know what is on the other side of the mountain and what is impossible with man is possible with you, Lord, only then will our faith be where God wants it, and we will walk on level ground.

The Nail

And he, bearing his cross, went out to a place called a place
of a skull which is called in Hebrew called Golgotha, where
they crucified him, and two others one on either side and
Jesus in the center.

—John 19:17

As me and my sister traveled back and forth on our journey with our
mother, the experience of a nail brought me and my sister to a place of
awe. Christ, in all his glory, appeared to us in a supernatural way again.

As we walk in the wake of cancer, God always takes us to a place of
the supernatural. We bow in awe of his magnificent tools of revealing
himself. My car was upon what appeared to us to be a large nail.

It should have been in my tire, but because of all the traffic, I did not
swerve and stayed on course. I said what a large nail and then I heard
my sister say it looked like a railroad tie; then we listened to a little sweet
voice from our mother say it was no nail; it was a stake at the Crucifixion
and then as a quickly as a flash the stake became real to me and in my
sister's mind.

We began to say yes, that was what it was like. My mother and I had
attended the Passion of the Christ before her diagnosis and watched with
no movement or coughing like had been going on with her.

When we arrived home, we discussed the nail, and she revealed, no, I never saw it in the road, so was it in the street, or was Christ telling her a route she would be traveling?

Was it meant for us to reassure us he is near and will be near us in our journey with our mother? Was it for us all in HIS revelation and peace for her to slip away in his arms to take her to Glory? O, what a Savior!

The Sting Of Death

O Death, where is your sting? O hades, where is your victory?

—1 Corinthians 15:55

Death, death, oh where is thy sting, yet Jesus, you have overcome the grave of death, and as the pain is real, so is the promise of our hope is confirmed, and your suffering at cavalry was not in vain.

You are present in the home today with every day closer for our mother to dwell in a place of peace, joy, no pain, and no worries of a world full of sin. We have watched a woman stand tall, face death as a mighty warrior, and talk of her death as though it is with joy. She longs, we see it, for this place where she wants to see all those who have gone before her, and she has traveled a long, hard road.

Losing a whole family and even daughters living away and no grand-children surrounding her life, she made lemonade with sour lemons. She was always there to fix grandchildren, make tea cakes, give quilts, and make each grandchild know they are loved.

She watched a world corrupt before her eyes in great-grandchildren suffering because of sin and hurts for her family who is in pain, but Jesus, you are using the pain to teach us all the power and love at the cross to teach us depending on you, not man.

It is a time like this that teaches strength and empowers us to face and take up the cross for each day, and if we fail, He will pick us up, and we will try again. He is a God who is faithful and a God who is merciful. God is all-knowing, provides a way, and knows all the circumstances. When we see a person, a phone call, or a card, we know you as close as we breathe.

May mercy be upon us all today as my mother, will be carried to a higher place, and your glory will be revealed to both of us, so Lord help our prayer to be thine on the way Lord, Have thine own way.

Where Is Your Bible?

Let no one deceive you with empty words for because of such things the wrath of God comes on those who are disobedient.

—Ephesians 5:6

Do you have a bible that is never opened because you are afraid to open your heart to hear words that might make you change? Maybe to open ourselves up to His voice, but we do not want to feel we lose control. It is our bible, one we like to interpret and remember words our parents and grandparents told us, so this is the bible we live by.

Do we get up hurrying off to work, not realizing He is the one who keeps you breathing and He is the one who allowed you to rise, and He is the one who gave you that job and blessed you with children and all the many things you take for granted?

Why do we get up every morning, making our list to do for the day, and the top priority is left off the list? If we would open the word, it would sweeten our voice, feed our spirits, and nourish our souls so that when we leave our door, we could stand the battleground of the day, war off Satan's tactics, and love our brother like Christ.

This society is so busy; the book lays still, the dust accumulates, and our hearts get a little more complicated daily; then we wonder why things aren't working. Like a plant, we walk by it, and if we never feed and water it, it will slowly die.

It lets you know it needs your attention by the signs, but we get so busy and in desperation, we try to keep it from dying then, and sometimes it is too late. Just like the Lord and His Word, our hearts may become so callous; we don't feel we need it, we don't see it or hear it, as it cries out to us, pick me up, and I'll meet all your needs.

It is like a road map for your life. We think because we get some of God growing up, we don't need Him when we can run our own life, but then we ask ourselves why, when life throws us a situation we cannot handle, is this happening to me and never realize they left God behind.

You invested in things that do not last and never had your hearts and minds filled with God's Word so you could cope with these deep valleys. We are not self-sufficient we are not God and not the Captain of our ship; Jesus is the captain.

We may come to the end of life and face an illness or some life event; then we will realize how much God's word we have and how much we know Him and may have regrets of lost time. He says to us daily to take up our cross.

If we failed yesterday, we could begin again today, so with all the hurricanes, tidal waves, tornadoes, fires, and earthquakes, we must wake up to the cry of this world because He told us in his word when you see the signs, the time growth near, so pick up the Word, empty your soul and fill it up with all God's promises and then and only then when you do this, you will stop and hear His voice say, "Look up, I am coming soon and I love you, please love me. I came to give you comfort and promises for your minds and hearts. Yet, you fret and stay so busy you run by me daily."

If we would only spend time together, how are you ever going to get to know me? We must learn and then go to others and share our hope, whether with our husbands, children, neighbors, or parents.

We cannot share it if we don't have the word in us, so Christ is calling loud and clear today: stop, turn around, be still, and only then will you feel his presence and feel the conviction of sin and the only then can we say, To God be the glory, great things He has done.

Who Understands Me Like You, Lord

Evildoers do not understand justice, but those who seek the Lord understand it all.

—Proverbs 28:5

Who can I go to that understands me like you, Lord, and knows what lies so deep within where I think, hurt, the agony that words cannot reveal, but what a friend I have in you, and you are the one who has suffered and was is the one who was rejected and felt all the emotional pain from betrayal and trying to do good and yet misunderstood.

As I sit today with losses and a strange stillness where everything and everyone has stopped and gone, Lord, I try to adjust to the loneliness and void where I had people all around, supporting me and caring.

When tragedy is over, and people go to the next drama, they do not understand we still need a hug, a call, a card even. Help me, Lord, to be a friend to someone who still needs a friend who cares, a little encouragement, a hug, and a smile.

You never got even, nor did you tell people all their faults. You hated sin and loved the sinner. Help me, Lord, my flesh has a hard time wanting to talk with this person and tell them I see them going in the wrong direction and making wrong decisions. You are a God who, in your word, said, " It is my battle, not yours, I'll repay vengeance is mine." Help me,

Lord, to be still, wait on you, and trust you more daily. Lord, help me go to the Rock that is higher than I.

Part Eight

Reflecting On The Holidays

Dear Reader,

Christmas and New Year—I have lived, loved, and enjoyed both holidays for decades. I love the traditions, the music, the food, the music, the family time, the gifts, but the meaning for me runs deeper. It's as if the world can stop its chaotic spinning and pause like a snapped photograph. As we look deeper into the image, we find Christ everywhere. He is the reason for the season and the reflection and hope of the New Year.

As we watch the world fall apart with our own eyes, we witness wars, famines, death, hatred, floods, droughts, earthquakes, and the destruction of morality. There is still hope. Why?

All of these mistakes, pain, fear, and lies have been paid for by the petite, gentle, innocent babe who lies in the manger. His life, the only life that can save us from spiritual and physical death, was born in a humble stable to two loving earthly parents who were charged to raise the Son of God for all of us.

May this short section stir your memories and love of the small babe, and may your heart swell with love and generosity to all around you.

A New Year And New Beginning

They will soar on wings like eagles; they will run and not grow weary. The Lord will renew their strength.

—Isaiah 40:31

A New Year's Day and a new beginning, Lord. You are a God of new beginnings. Old things are unique to you. It is a journey for us all, and choices have brought us to a new year, whether right or wrong.

We can use the past as stepping stones and wisdom to make wiser choices, continue in our sameness, and never grow or change if we do not step out of our box and go where the Lord leads.

Can we, in our strength, do it right, or can we choose a Savior who can make it right so we can make better choices? We have so much confusion because we have run to the world and all of its glitz because we think we are the captain of our ship.

The Lord lets us drive, and when the waves get high, and we cannot have control any longer, we scream for help. Do we look for the lighthouse and anchor, which is the Lord, when all else fails, or do we, in our stubborn hearts, keep steering our ships until the waves take us down to the depth where there is no return?

We become so occupied with our control that we fail to chart our course and just start life without consulting the one who has the map of life. He charts our system and is the compass and lighthouse; only then will we reach our destination.

His ways, not our ways, a choice that seems right to man but the wrong way to the Lord. Why do we think we do not have to consult our tour guide in life when if we were taking a cruise, we plan, make reservations, and want to know what island and even every detail of our trip?

We never plan the trip to eternity, take time to make our reservation to heaven, or read our map, which is God's word. This word would chart our course, His plan, and His will for our life. Why do we never realize there is a final destination, just like a return on our cruise, all because we do not want to let go of the world and all its lure of things?

When our hearts are broken, and the pain of life appears like a storm in the "Big Easy," then we scream, "where is God?" If we would be still, read the map, stay on course, and let Christ, who created the sea and knows every wave that turns and how to calm the sea and our fears, then we would have this peace we all yearn so desperately to have.

As *Auld Lang Syne* sings, "I will have it my way when society should be singing. Have thine own way, Lord, so we will continue to search." The world will become more like Sodom and Gomorrah all because we have become a lost people on a lost sea and ship of people tossing and turning and yet never yielding the rudder to the one who has the experience and knows our fears and longing to get back to the shore.

We must lay our tired bodies down and deliver to a Captain who can take us to places we have never been. We need to see where He will take us, and then we may enjoy this ride called life. We learn to say to Him, "Thank you for the trip." We will say, "How much I owe you?" And He will say, "I have paid everything."

We learn who is in charge, then peace will flood our souls, and like an eagle, we will soar higher and rise to new heights that only knowing a Savior can accomplish. "Not our will, Lord, but your will be done." The past is the past, and the future is today with our choices. To God be the glory of great things He has done.

Christmas Without Love

For God so loved the world that he gave his only begotten Son that whoever believes on him will be saved.

—John 3:16

What happened to families and love? Where is love and concern for one another and one who sticks closer than a brother? We watch TV shows like *Leave It to Beaver* and Christmas, and families are glad to see each other. When the real world is lived, I wonder why ours is lacking love.

Where is all the laughter and fun we once had as children and all around with excitement? Our world prepares for shopping, gifts, wrapping, cooking, and parties, and we are exhausted before the big day arrives. Then we are so disappointed when someone we love cannot attend, the loneliness of all our losses kick in, death, or maybe an event that just doesn't fit in at the happy holiday season.

We set ourselves up with unrealistic expectations that disappoint us, so we, in the blink of an eye, unwrap, run here and there, opening all the surprises, and when it is over, it is like a rush of mixed emotions, one of what can we do now or the I'm glad it is over. We want to get it behind us, and then, if we had stopped, paused, and remembered love for Christ, love for each other, and maybe forgiveness to be invited to the gathering, the family would become whole and fellowship sweet.

When hearts have become calloused and so hard that when strangers are treated better than our own, then we must examine our life and ask what am I holding on to that should be laid at the feet of the cross and ask for a mind and heart that loves all people around not just our own.

We never realize that the Lord hates idols, and when we worship our family more than Him, our Lord is a jealous God. Many houses this Christmas will feel a fleet of momentary excitement, and in the blink of an eye, it is all over, and if we ever learn that Christ, His love, His peace, and it is all about Him.

When we get Him in the correct order, then each person who comes through our doors or when we go to another's home, we will reflect Christmas because when Christ changes our hearts and cleanses us from all the wrong in our life, then the motives, the attitudes and the fruit of our spirit will be evident. The light will shine, and we will not need to say Merry Christmas.

It will be revealed in our love of one another. Until we look for Christmas inward and not outward; only then will we ever know the true meaning of Christmas. When we get to see the baby who grew up to be a man and died for us, and only then when the Holy Spirit comes to live in your heart, who comforts, protects, and guides our ways, will we learn to say Merry Christmas with true meaning and not just words that are expected.

The lights on the tree are more beautiful, the gifts because of the sacrifice Christ gave, and the happiness and joy all are symbols of a baby's birth, so then a depth of love will flow toward each other and like never before, and peace in your home will reign and remain.

Christmas is about love and a time for Jesus, not a time for malls and all the world's lures. When all sins are confessed, repentant hearts are changed, and when we wish each other Merry Christmas, we will feel the warmth like a fire burning, and we will all know this truly is a real MERRY CHRISTMAS.

Forgotten Birthday

What credit is that to you if you love those who love you?
Even sinners love those who love them.

—Luke 6:32

Today, Lord, is your birthday, and yet I see a generation asking and receiving and rushing to get and yet cannot slow down to receive a gift that will last eternally and the only gift that will give peace and joy to our hearts, that ribbons and decorations that will not last only to be trashed soon, and yet w never utter the name, Jesus.

Families torn apart because of selfishness, greed, and hurt go to the grave and miss the abundant life of what Christmas was given to give. When Christ is removed from our hearts and energy and replaced with money and things that fade away like dust that settles on the earth, time goes by, and loved ones are now grown older and maybe gone, then we realize what all we invested our time and those things we should have done will not be able to be regained, then the regrets of our hearts appear.

We must daily live for a Jesus who breathed life into our being and had a plan for all of us, and only then will we be able to have a hole inside us filled, and love radiates to each person we meet. Repentance of the past and love for each other now, and then we will know who holds our future.

Lord, this has been, I would call, a whirlwind Christmas, every child going to different functions and not taking the time to hear from each other's hearts and get to know what will carry us through the storms of life. How do we reach young people if they do not slow down from all the lure of the world and take time to hear the name of Jesus and that He is the answer to all their hurts and disappointments?

If your word is never explored and revealed, we must let them see a Christ in us so they can know something different in our lives and homes. We must love like you, Lord, see like you, hear like you, and think with sound minds that can only be given by the most incredible gift-givers.

This Christmas was rushed and frantic, but with a family with so many homes to attend; I will let go, Lord, and know that I've tried to express your love and give love through me, so Lord, let me wish you a happy birthday and thank you for all you have done and given to me.

You are a loving God, and I praise you for it all. To God be the glory, great things you have done, and sorry we rushed your party and made you feel not welcomed, and yet it was your birthday party, and nobody ever realized you were here.

Did we fail to open your gift, Lord, and in the hurry of getting and giving, did we forget to be still and hear from you, so forgive us for ignoring you and rushing you out? Every day is Christmas, so help us all to think differently about your birthday and the meaning of Christmas.

Jesus Not Rabbits

I am the resurrection and the life. The one who believes in me shall live.

—John 11:25

Secret thoughts and secret lives are found in each person we face. Many live and express themselves and soon reveal a spiritual oneness with Christ or a sensual nature, which reveals itself soon as the mouth speaks. We only see the outside, and it doesn't take long when a person tells their heart and soul.

We all want a quick fix or a band-aid and do not want to do the hard stuff in life. If we can buy, spend the money, and drown out a voice that screams our name and a restlessness of soul, then we do not change or feel the need to change, so we think we win at this game of life.

When children are raised by parents with this mindset, it produces a generation of hurting and confused individuals and sometimes angry children and adults. As those who watch from a distance, we see the signs and become alarmed at what these children may develop with these role models.

This is Easter, and rabbits are not symbols or colored eggs; it is all about Jesus. The young adult parents are teaching a generation of children. Easter is about attending Church once a year and wearing a new outfit, and rabbits and eggs replace Jesus and the tomb. As we monitor the shelves of department stores, it is all geared toward baskets, rabbits, and eggs.

As we face another Easter, Jesus is alive, and are we telling the little children that Jesus arose, and He lives now and to learn the story of His love, or do rabbits, eggs, presents, replace one who died in order we may live and gives families, and children hope for this world of war, sin, and war against anything resembles Christ.

Adults act out destructive behaviors and dysfunction around the children across this nation while children deal with homes with strangers; confused children ask where they belong in this world and what is safe. We see children having the crumbs from the life of parents, maybe no hugs, no kisses, no fun game, no laughter, only a T.V. DVD, and learning to be a make-believe character mixed with some acted-out aggression. It doesn't take long when our televisions reveal a society gone badly.

When Jesus is removed from our homes, we allow satan to lead the children into a dark world of no return. Young adult parents then wonder why the teenager is acting so badly and never coming to terms with how their home was acted out before them, and they mimic a lifestyle, whether it be drinking, drugs, sex, and on and on.

When young adult parents face the truth, the truth will never set them free, there will never be peace, and children's emotional lives will be destroyed. One day, at the end of it all, and we face Christ face to face, we will all deal with the consequences of bad choices.

Our children and grandchildren act out a behavior that was acted out before them, and we will ask ourselves, did we teach them Jesus, or did not ourselves know this one who gives peace and joy and an abundant life? Instead of searching for eggs and chocolate bunnies, maybe explore the scripture and our souls, find what this easter is all about, and let Jesus fill our Easter baskets.

Life Is But A Vapor

My age is nothing before you, certainly, every man at his best state is but a vapor.

—Psalm 39:5

How did I get to the age of my parents so quickly? Time can rush us forward, whether we want to go or not. We might say things like, "I'll do that tomorrow." Then, tomorrow never comes, and regrets of yesterday loom, so here we are before a mirror, seeing our faces of many years and yet inward renewing and outward fading away of our youth and yet a joy we never thought would ever come to know.

Investing in lives, investing in love, and investing in time grows interest and cannot ever be robbed by man, and I am reminded that the Lord is my security. He's all the security I need, and he's all I want. The things on earth grow strangely dim when we grow with the Lord.

Why do we doubt his word when he, like a real father, means what he says? Why do we think Jesus died a death like he did not be taken lightly as a people? He loved us and did not want us to waste these years called life. Spending time with one another gets us to know each other intimately. Yet, we never have an intimate relationship with him because we never cease our labor and take time to read his word and get to know this holy spirit in us who resides in us when we accepted Christ.

I want to influence my children and grandchildren and tell them they need a savior. When tragedy strikes, and lousy news comes, an ache in our heart beyond repair by man, we must have an anchor that does not move and secures us so we will not be forced.

Gifts, trees, and lights are all in a moment of joy, so why don't we take the advantage that lasts? And every day, we will enjoy Christmas with the Greatest friend, the most excellent relative, one who never disappoints, one who never hurts us, one who loves us no matter what, one who can heal, help, and give us answers that man cannot reach.

Man is just like us, human & flesh and sin, so why do we think the security is in people, trips, houses, cars and things when the one who is the great provider of all these things wants us to enjoy our journey and wants us to have an abundant life, but not to use his gifts as idols that lure our minds and hearts from him.

We must never forget Christmas: why the baby was born, and why he came to die and get to know the lord of lords and king of kings. When all else fails, and it will, it will all let you down sooner or later. Still, the one who never forgets you nor rejects you will take your life to higher places you have never been before.

If we all come to honor him, seek him, worship him, love him, and anything we need to know, he will provide only when our hearts have been repented, cleansed, become obedient, and set our priorities in order.

Again, we get past our youth very quickly, reach where we must face ourselves in the mirror, and then decide who we worship, self or Christ born in a manger and died on an old rugged cross, and choose how we'll live the remaining days. Some days, we can run and escape the reality of life where we are, but we will never escape the one big decision when we breathe our last breath: which way will we go?

We don't want to wait until then to know a Christ who gave His all; He only wants us to provide our all. Then Christmas will remain in our hearts and lives every year, and we'll reflect His spirit inside us, and His birth and death will not be in vain.

Christmas is love and giving, so what will we give each other? I want a Jesus who gave His all; I want my heart to feel more love, sharing, and forgiving, and may Christmas remain in me through Christ and His sacrifice. Amen

Part Nine

Poems

Dear Reader,

What Is Poetry? Are Psalms poetry? Both come from the heart with words and structure that tell the reader about words' emotional, concentrated, lyrical impact. I have done that in these four poems from my heart.

I pray you will feel the impact of the words and that God can use them to stir your heart and soul to change, seek Him, forgive yourself, and love others. In the end, that is what it's all about—finding God and loving our neighbors as ourselves.

A Servant

I no longer call you servant because a servant does not know His master's business. Instead, I have called you friend for everything I have learned from my father.

—John 15:15

As I become your servant
I have been tested all the way
I look at this one whom I serve
And ask, do I have strength today?

But you poured enough love into my heart
And you ask me loud and clear
Do you love me today, my child?
As I hold this one so dear.

She came to me so many times
And poured her heart out loud.
Then, when she screamed , please pray.
With our heads, we bowed.

I hold her close to my bosom with love.
But all I could do was reach above.
She then began to calm her fears
I covered this one;only to show my love

If she only knew the love I have
And all the pain I have been through
Do you ever think when you read this
Because this could all be you.

I have tried not to hurt, only to love.
have tried to serve my Lord.
I have tried to be his servant
And be in one accord.

Only you, Lord, will ever know.
The amount of pain I had.
And when I get to heaven
At that point, I knew I would be glad.

So I will try to serve you to the end, my Lord
I cannot quit now for you.
For I will love and serve others
how what only you can really do.

Man Can Not Understand

Create in me a clean heart, Oh God.

—Psalm 51:10

If only those near and dear to us
Could only understand
The groans and heartaches that we feel.
To a certain extent, they can.

We try so many times to communicate
Our feelings that lie so deep
We only get some understanding.
So you, Lord, I will seek

I, now in agony, reveal it al
And realize in all you now know
The struggle inside with my flesh.
Your love for me, you show

Even those who are closest to us
Who will never understand?
What agony and pain that we bear?
Because they are human and man

So to you, Lord, I will carry my burden
The dependence on man is gone.
I am in this valley this time, Lord
Just you and me alone.

My Alter

I will not violate my covenant or alter what my lips have uttered; no, I will not break my covenant; I will not take back a single word.

—Psalm 89:34

I made myself an altar.
In the corner of my room
To go to my sweet Jesus
It is joy not of doom.

I listen to music.
That lifts my heart each day.
Then, as I felt his presence
I began to really pray.

I then have a feeling that overtakes me.
I then began to write.
I praise my wonderful Jesus.
I hope I never lose sight.

I feel so very peaceful.this day
I feel close to my Lord.
I know there is a reason.
Why has he asked me to carry this sword?

There is a sweet, sweet spirit.
Inside me, never like this before
I was seeking, knocking, and asking
He led me through the door.

Oh what is my Savior doing?
I will never understand it all.
But I know I have learned to lean
He catches me when I fall.

So, I am at the altar.
Only to praise him and ask the way
Only to ask him and say to him
Have your way with me, and watch what I say.

What If The Baby Had Not Been Born

This is how the birth of Jesus the Messiah came about. His mother pledged to be married to Joseph, but before they came together, she was with child by the Holy Spirit.

—Luke 2:18

What if that little baby
Never laid in the manger for me
What if my Jesus never died?
So love us to see

Oh, glory to his name.
Oh, praise him. He did rise
And because he lives
There, my soul now lies.

There are times
That I know he is with me
When I hurt, and pain is felt.
I am exactly where all along I should be

Then, when he takes control
And lifts me deep within
He assures, and he holds me
And forgives all my sin.

Sometimes, in a crisis
We do what we think is right
But to another
It leads only to a fight.

So you see, I hear God saying
Loudly in my ear once again today
Don't act upon yourself, my child
Do it all for me and my way

So desperately I come seeking.
A feeling of release
And praise God, he hears, and he answers
And all the pain has ceased.

So when there is no other
You can go with it all
Please listen to this message
On Jesus, you can call.

Epilogue

Dear Reader,

As the last word fell from this book on your conscious thought, I hoped to share a secret. I now stand in the whole light. I made it through the darkest, most challenging time to the other side. My life felt like I was cruising along on a raised bridge over troubled water when the road beneath my tires suddenly gave way, plunging my vehicle into the blackest deep. With the force of the fall, troubled waters poured in through the smashed glass I thought would protect me.

Suddenly, with the car filling up, survival mode kicked in. I unbuckled and swam through the sinking vehicle to the water's surface, breaking through at the very last second when my lungs were about to burst.

I gulped in substantial lungs full of air while my legs and arms treaded the black, murky water to keep me afloat. Distressed, I tried to navigate where I was. Could I see where I had come from? Was the bridge still around? I could only see a dark, stormy horizon of rolling black water. What choice did I have other than to swim through this storm of life?

The winds of confusion had picked up, causing the waves to break against me. I felt my body begin awkwardly swimming against the waves, but I was unsure what direction to start. "Dear God, help me—save me!" I prayed. I waited to hear the still, small voice whisper directions in the deep—nothing.

I bobbed, sank, and surfaced a few desperate times with the same prayer—crying out, saying, "I am trying to give my all, and all is not good enough." It felt like I was at the bottom of the ocean floor crying, saying, "This is as low as I can go; only you, Lord, can lift me up from here. I love the people around me and do not want to hurt anyone." Suddenly, as those words left my mouth, I felt hope. I felt like someone was there beside me. It was Jesus.

With Jesus as my guide, support, and lifeline, the waves of trouble tumbled me in non-rhythmically randomness, but instead of downing, I was supplied with air. With His help, I always surfaced.

I indeed gasped for air more than once, and then I felt the crushing tsunami slam me with the force of 10,000 gallons of despair. The salty tears filled my lungs and sinuses as grief nearly engulfed me. But again, I would bob to the top just enough to take in a breath of air.

For years, this cycle continued until one day, I was spit out onto the sands of life with the waves of pain just licking my feet. Water dripped off my head and down my face as my chest heaved, filling my lungs with the breath of life—I was going to make it.

Readers, I have made it through the pain of abandonment and betrayal, which were the damaged emotions I had inside. I felt hopeless with two small children 700 miles from my roots; All I could do was go out at midnight and cry out to GOD.

Little did I know there were secrets behind the scenes that contributed to the family's feelings acting out in the way they only knew to survive the shock of the unexpected death of the father and the Mother leaving six months later. The excruciating pain of those years of loss and grief placed me to know the Savior in my extremities—and He brought me out.

Through that experience, I gained a vast amount of wisdom and humility that I apply to life today. As the world crashes down around us at an unprecedented rate, I know that no matter the heartache or pain, He is there to bless and comfort me. I pray that you will be filled with that knowledge and that this book contributed to it somehow.

I hope you find your way to the Lord like the children of Israel when they crossed the Red Sea. When your foot goes into the deep water and you hold Jesus' hand, then come to the other side as a person like Jesus wants you to be. You must accept His help, trust Him, and know Him. I hope, one day, to meet you and give you a smile and a hug, knowing you can make it. God is there to help—always.

Printed in the USA
CPSIA information can be obtained
at www.ICGtesting.com
LVHW090725160624
783329LV00001B/8